Crash Course in Visual Basic™ 3

Ken Miller
Allen Wyatt
Mike Shinkel

Crash Course in Visual Basic™ 3

Copyright© 1994 by Que® Corporation

Library of Congress Catalog No.: 94-65523

ISBN: 1-56529-765-2

97 96 95 94   4 3 2 1

Interpretation of the printing code: the rightmost double-digit number is the year of the book's printing; the rightmost single-digit number, the number of the book's printing. For example, a printing code of 94-1 shows that the first printing of the book occurred in 1994.

Publisher: David P. Ewing

Associate Publisher: Michael Miller

Publishing Director: Joseph B. Wikert

Managing Editor: Michael Cunningham

Product Marketing Director: Ray Robinson

Credits

Publishing Manager
Brad Koch

Acquisitions Editor
Angela J. Lee

Product Director
Bryan Gambrel

Production Editor
Judy Brunetti

Technical Editors
Patrick Irwin
D.F. Scott

Acquisitions Coordinator
Patricia Brooks

Book Designer
Amy Peppler-Adams

Graphic Image Specialists
Teresa Forrester
Tim Montgomery
Dennis Sheehan
Sue VandeWalle

Production Team
Angela Bannan
Jodie Cantwell
Karen Dodson
Terri Edwards
Brook Farling
Jeanne Lemen
Elizabeth Lewis
Aren Munk
G. Alan Palmore
Caroline Roop
Donna Winter
Michael Thomas

Indexer
Charlotte Clapp
Johnna VanHoose

Composed in *Stone Serif* and *MCPdigital*
by Que Corporation

About the Authors

Kenneth Miller has been designing and programming computers since 1975 when, at the age of 15, he built his first microcomputer—based on an Intel 8080. He has a Bachelor's degree in Electrical Engineering, a Master's degree in Business Administration, and is a licensed Professional Engineer. Kenneth currently spends most of his time programming in Visual Basic and Visual C++. His CompuServe address is 73504,1240.

Allen Wyatt, a recognized expert in small computer systems, has been working in the computer and publishing industries for more than 15 years. He has written almost 30 books about all facets of working with computers—from programming to using application software to operating systems. The books he has written and worked on have helped millions of people. Allen is the president of Discovery Computing Inc., a computer and publishing services company in Sundance, Wy. He lives with his wife and three children on a 350-acre ranch just outside of town, on the edge of the Black Hills. In his spare time, he tends his animals, has fun with his family, and participates in church and community events.

Mike Shinkel calls Atlanta, Ga., home. He is president of Expert Education, Inc., a training and consulting firm that specializes in business application development software, and president of VBxtras, Inc., a catalog software sales company that specializes in Visual Basic add-on products. Mike authored *Programming in Clipper 5*, published by Addison-Wesley; he writes the Q&A column for *Clipper Advisor* magazine; he has spoken at more than a dozen computer conferences throughout the world; and he frequently writes articles about development tools for business applications. You can get a copy of the Visual Basic add-on products catalog, *VBxtras*, by calling 800-788-4794 or 404-952-6388.

Trademark Acknowledgments

Que Corporation has made every attempt to supply trademark information about company names, products, and services mentioned in this book. Trademarks indicated were derived from various sources. Que Corporation cannot attest to the accuracy of this information.

We'd Like To Hear From You!

As part of our continuing effort to produce books of the highest possible quality, Que would like to hear your comments. To stay competitive, we *really* want you, as a computer book reader and user, to let us know what you like or dislike most about this book or other Que products.

You can mail comments, ideas, or suggestions for improving future editions to the address below, or send us a fax at (317) 581-4663. For the on-line inclined, Macmillan Publishing now has a forum on CompuServe (type **GO QUEBOOKS** at any prompt) through which our staff and authors are available for questions and comments. In addition to exploring our forum, please feel free to contact me personally on CompuServe at 74143,1574 to discuss your opinions of this book.

Thanks in advance—your comments will help us to continue publishing the best books available on computer topics in today's market.

Bryan Gambrel
Product Development Specialist
Que Corporation
201 W. 103rd Street
Indianapolis, Indiana 46290
USA

Contents at a Glance

Introduction 1

1 The Visual Basic Environment 5
2 Creating Forms 31
3 Adding Functionality 47
4 Variables and Operators 71
5 Using Built-In Functions 93
6 Controlling Program Flow 125
7 Using Data Structures 141
8 Dialog Boxes 157
9 Debugging 175
10 File Handling 193

Index 223

Contents

Introduction   **1**

   Who Should Use This Book? 1
   Syntax at a Glance 2
   Conventions Used 3

1 The Visual Basic Environment   **5**

   Minimum Requirements 5
   Starting Visual Basic 6
   Parts of the Environment 7
      The Form 7
      The Menu Bar 8
      The Toolbar 10
      The Project Window 11
      The Toolbox 12
      The Properties Window 15
   Getting Help 16
      Searching for Help 17
      Navigating the Help System 18
      Your Own Private Tutor 19
      Learning by Example 19
   Customizing Visual Basic 20
      Environment Options 20
      Project Options 21
   Your First Visual Basic Program 22
      Creating the Program 22
      Drawing the Interface 23
      Running Your Program 27
      Saving Your Work 28
   Quitting Visual Basic 28
   Adding Your Program to a Group 28
   From Here... 29

2 Creating Forms   **31**

   Adding a New Form 31
   Changing Appearance and Behavior 32
   Types of Properties 33
   Properties Related to Forms 33
      Color Properties 34
      Text Properties 36
      Size and Location Properties 37
      BorderStyle 38
      Visible 39
      The Control Menu 39
      Picture Properties 40
      WindowState 42
      Other Properties 42

Revisiting the Calculator 42
  Opening the Project 42
  Making Changes to the Form 43
  Testing the Result 44
From Here... 44

3 Adding Functionality   47

Your Toolbox 47
Working with Controls 48
  Changing Control Properties 49
  Moving Controls 51
  Resizing Controls 51
  Copying Controls 52
  Deleting Controls 53
Commonly Used Controls 53
  Command Buttons 53
  Labels 54
  Text Boxes 55
  Check Boxes 56
  Option Buttons 56
  Grouping Controls 57
  Scroll Bars 59
  Listing Information 60
Control Properties 64
  Caption 64
  Text 65
  Text Box Properties 65
  Appearance of Your Text 66
  Alignment 67
  Value 68
  Enabled 68
  Visible 68
  The Tab Order 69
From Here... 69

4 Variables and Operators   71

Understanding Data Types 71
  Standard Variable Types 73
  Integer 73
  Special Data Types 76
  Variable Declarations 77
Understanding Operators 81
  Arithmetic Operators 81
  Comparison Operators 84
  Logical Operators 86
  String Operators 91
From Here... 91

5 Using Built-In Functions   93

The Benefits of Functions 93
Date and Time Functions 94
  How Visual Basic Stores Dates and Times 95

Determining Today's Date 96
Determining the Current Time 96
Getting Both the Time and Date 97
Extracting Part of the Date 99
Extracting Part of the Time 99
Differences Between Two Dates 100
Deriving a Date 104
String Functions 105
Comparing Strings 108
Converting Strings 109
Creating Strings 112
Other String Functions 113
Finding the Length of a String 113
Strings Within Strings 114
Math Functions 115
Extracting an Integer 116
Generating Random Numbers 116
Determining the Sign of a Number 118
Positive Values 118
Formatting 119
Miscellaneous Functions 120
Sounding Off 120
Cooperating With Windows 121
From Here… 124

6 Controlling Program Flow   125

Conditional Execution 125
If...Then 126
Select Case 129
Switch 131
Looping Structures 132
While...Wend 133
Do...Loop 134
For...Next 136
GoTo 139
From Here… 140

7 Using Data Structures   141

Understanding Arrays 141
Setting Up an Array 142
Changing Arrays on the Fly 144
Multidimensional Arrays 144
User-Defined Data Types 146
Getting Information About an Array 147
Starting to Count 150
Searching 151
Sorting 152
Substitution Sort 153
QuickSort 154
From Here… 155

8 Dialog Boxes   157

Creating a Message Box 157
  The Message 158
  The Title 160
  Icons, Buttons, and Responses 161
  Modality 164
Getting User Input 165
  The Prompt 166
  The Title 167
  Default Input 168
  Screen Coordinates 169
Custom Dialog Boxes 169
  Creating the Dialog Box 169
  Additional Features 170
  Locating the Dialog Box 171
  Displaying Dialog Boxes 172
From Here… 174

9 Debugging   175

What Are Bugs? 175
  Syntax-Related Errors 176
  Logic-Related Errors 176
  Operation-Related Errors 176
Why Are Bugs a Problem? 177
  Keeping Bugs Out 178
  What is Debugging? 179
Getting Rid of Bugs 180
  Single Stepping 182
  Breakpoints 185
  Watch Expressions 188
From Here… 191

10 File Handling   193

File Types 193
  ASCII Text Files 194
  Foreign File Formats 196
  Import/Export Formats 196
  Initialization (.INI) Files 197
File Basics 198
  Opening a File 198
  Handling File Errors 200
  Reading Data Files 200
  Closing Files 201
  Loading a File 202
Types of File Access 203
  Sequential Files 203
  Random-Access Files 209
  Binary Files 215
Updating .INI Files 219
From Here… 221

Index   223

Introduction

Put on your crash helmets and get ready to learn Visual Basic fast! *Crash Course in Visual Basic* is one of several books in Que's series of "Crash Course" titles. The philosophy of these books is a simple one: You can learn a new programming language without much "fluff" getting in your way. This book is a tutorial of the Visual Basic language, packed with command descriptions and format syntax. Although *Crash Course in Visual Basic* is a concise book, it offers numerous examples of code. It also explains the more difficult concepts in enough detail to understand the underlying ideas. By reading *Crash Course in Visual Basic*, you will begin to reap the rewards of Visual Basic programming in a very short time.

Who Should Use This Book?

If you have programmed before but are new to Visual Basic, this book will help you become a Visual Basic programmer. In today's fast-paced world, people do not have much time to spend learning new skills. Adding a programming language to your bag of tricks can be useful both on the job and at home. Visual Basic offers the advantage of working with the world's most popular graphical user interface (GUI): Microsoft Windows. With this book, Visual Basic, and Windows, you have everything you need to begin writing Visual Basic programs.

If you are new to programming, or new to programming in the Windows environment, but feel you can master programming concepts without too much trouble, this book is intended for you as well. You will find that major concepts, such as drawing a Windows interface or editing and running a Visual Basic program, are fully explained hand-in-hand with putting Visual Basic skills to work. You will find this approach both instructive and productive.

The only real expectation of you, as the reader, is that you know how to *use* Windows—you don't need to know how to program in Windows, only how to use it. Visual Basic relies very heavily on the Windows user interface, and a firm understanding of how to use the mouse, windows, pull-down menus, and dialog boxes is essential to feeling comfortable with this book.

Syntax at a Glance

Crash Course in Visual Basic features a how-to approach that briefly explains why a command is important, and then provides one or two short code examples to illustrate the important features of each command. Throughout each chapter, you'll see shaded boxes named *Syntax at a Glance*. These boxes contain important information, making *Crash Course in Visual Basic* an extremely valuable resource—a resource you can return to throughout your Visual Basic programming career. A sample Syntax at a Glance box follows:

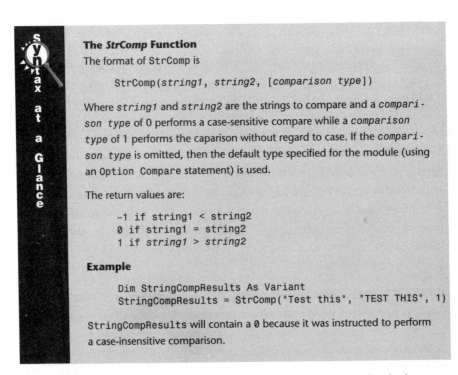

The *StrComp* Function

The format of StrComp is

    StrComp(*string1*, *string2*, [*comparison type*])

Where *string1* and *string2* are the strings to compare and a *comparison type* of 0 performs a case-sensitive compare while a *comparison type* of 1 performs the caparison without regard to case. If the *comparison type* is omitted, then the default type specified for the module (using an Option Compare statement) is used.

The return values are:

    -1 if string1 < string2
    0 if string1 = string2
    1 if *string1* > *string2*

Example

    Dim StringCompResults As Variant
    StringCompResults = StrComp("Test this", "TEST THIS", 1)

StringCompResults will contain a 0 because it was instructed to perform a case-insensitive comparison.

Besides Syntax at a Glance boxes, you will find three other visual aids that can help you on your Visual Basic journey.

> **Note**
>
> Note boxes provide you with additional information. This information helps speed your learning and reminds you of important information that bears repeating.

> **Caution**
>
> Caution boxes warn you of problem areas, including procedures that can possibly harm your computer or cause your program not to run.

Tip

Tip boxes offer possible ideas for shortcuts and hints to make programming in Visual Basic easier and more efficient.

Conventions Used

To get the most out of this book, you should know how it is designed. The following list introduces you to the general conventions used in this book:

- New terms and emphasized words appear in *italics*.

- Statements, commands, functions, and so on appear in a special `monospace` typeface.

- Anything you are asked to type appears in **bold**. Responses to program prompts appear in `monospace bold`.

- If you are given information about which menu choices to make, the hot keys for the menu items are shown in bold, as in "choose **O**pen Project from the **F**ile menu."

- In code lines, placeholders—words that represent text you insert— appear in `monospace italic`. For example, `filename` or `variable`.

- In syntax lines, brackets ([]) indicate optional items. Do not type the brackets when you include these parameters in your programs.

- Some lines of Visual Basic code are too long to fit within the margins of this book. A special line-wrap icon (➡) is used to indicate when two or more lines in the book are typed as one line in your program.

Without any further delay, turn the page and begin your journey towards mastering the Visual Basic language.

Chapter 1

The Visual Basic Environment

Visual Basic (sometimes abbreviated simply as VB) offers a simple approach to programming for the Windows environment. With Visual Basic, you can quickly and easily create programs that combine a professional appearance with powerful features that allow you to take full advantage of your computer system.

In this chapter, you will start your crash course in using Visual Basic. You will learn what you need to run a program you construct, how you can take advantage of the environment, and some basic commands that you will use whenever you use VB. You will even create your first Visual Basic program—not bad after only one chapter! You will start by examining what you will need to fully exploit Visual Basic's capabilities.

Minimum Requirements

Before you can install Visual Basic on your computer, your hardware and software must meet certain minimum requirements. After you start developing programs with Visual Basic, you may decide to give or sell your programs to others. Any computer system on which these programs are executed must also meet these requirements:

- 80286 CPU or higher

- Windows 3.1 or later

- 1M or more of system memory

- Approximately 30M of free hard drive space

These are the *minimum* requirements. Any seasoned computer user knows, however, that there is a distinct difference between minimum requirements and *recommended* requirements. For example, if you want to *really* use Visual Basic effectively, you should also have the following:

- A mouse

- A VGA or SVGA video system

- 4M of memory

Most computers sold within the last few years meet these minimum and recommended requirements. In fact, if your computer was supplied with Windows, you can run Visual Basic or virtually any program developed with VB. Why? Because the minimum requirements to run Windows are at least as great as those required to run Visual Basic.

After you have determined that you have the proper system to run Visual Basic, you should install the program according to the instructions in the user's reference manual. If you have installed Windows programs before, you can probably get by without referring to this manual. Just follow the steps listed on the label for Disk 1, the Setup disk.

Tip
If you are not yet in Windows, you can start both Windows and Visual Basic in one step. From the DOS command line, simply type **VB** and press Enter. Windows loads automatically, and you are taken directly to the Visual Basic system. (Successful use of this tip assumes that the Visual Basic program, VB.EXE, is in the current directory or a directory specified by your DOS PATH statement.)

After you've launched SETUP.EXE, then as the Setup program proceeds, answer the questions which appear on-screen. Make sure you allow anywhere from 15 minutes to an hour to do the installation. The actual time you use depends on the speed of your computer and how quickly you answer the questions. After you have successfully installed Visual Basic, you are ready to start using the program.

Starting Visual Basic

There are a variety of ways you can start Visual Basic. The easiest way to start Visual Basic, if you are already in Windows, is by double-clicking the VB program icon in the Visual Basic program group of the Program Manager. You can, however, use any of the other ways to start a Windows program, including the following:

- Double-click VB.EXE in the File Manager.

- Choose **R**un from the **F**ile menu in the Program Manager and then enter **VB.EXE** (along with its installed path) at the command line.

Regardless of how you start Visual Basic, you will see several different items appear on your screen. Together these items represent the Visual Basic environment. Figure 1.1 shows an example of how your screen may appear.

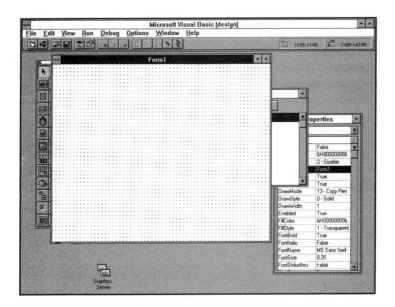

Fig. 1.1
What you see after starting Visual Basic.

Parts of the Environment

Unlike many other Windows programs, Visual Basic overlays whatever you have on your screen. For example, notice that the regular Windows desktop is still visible in the background of figure 1.1. This approach to building a screen can be confusing, particularly to beginners. Don't let it throw you, however. Just remember that there are only a few main *elements* to the Visual Basic environment.

Each element used in the VB development environment performs a valuable function. In the following sections, you will explore each of these elements and find out their purpose.

The Form

The most prominent element of the Visual Basic environment is the blank form that appears right in the middle of your screen. (The form is shown in figure 1.2.) Forms simply describe how the window screen will look when your Visual Basic program is running. When you create a form you are, in effect, developing your own program windows. Because almost all applications written in Visual Basic include at least one form, Visual Basic's way of getting you started is to present a blank form that you can start to use right away.

Fig. 1.2
A blank form.

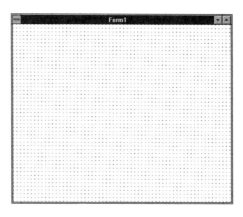

Later in this chapter, you will actually develop a real Visual Basic program in which you will work with the Form window. For now, however, you are just learning some parts of the Visual Basic environment. It is probably a good idea if you close the form so it does not block other elements of the screen. You do this by clicking the control-menu icon in the upper-left corner of the form. (This is the same way you close any window within Windows.)

The Menu Bar
The *menu bar* is the row of text under Visual Basic's title bar, as shown in figure 1.3. You can select menus with either the mouse or the keyboard. To select a menu with the mouse, just point to the menu name and click the left button. A pull-down menu appears. Using the keyboard, however, requires a little more information.

Fig. 1.3
The menu bar appears at the top of your screen.

Notice that the first character of each menu name in the menu bar is underlined. The underlined character is the *access key* for that menu. In some other programs, these access keys are often called *hot keys*. To activate a menu, press and hold the Alt key and then press the relative access key. For example, to pull down the **F**ile menu, press and hold the Alt key and then press F.

After you pull down a menu, notice that each menu item also has an access key. Unlike the menu names, the access key for a menu item isn't always the first letter. This is because many menu items start with the same letters. If the first letter was always underlined, then the access keys wouldn't be unique. The access key would still work—Windows would simply cycle through all the menu items using that particular access key, highlighting each of them in turn. To execute a particular item, you would have to press the Enter key. For rapid access, reduced confusion, and ease of use, other letters in the menu item are defined as the access key instead. The underlined letter within a menu item is always the access key for that menu item.

Selecting a menu item using an access key is even easier than selecting a menu. Just press the access key *without* pressing the Alt key. For example, to select the **N**ew Project menu item, while the **F**ile menu is open, press N without using Alt. What could be faster?

Shortcut keys! As their name implies, *shortcut keys* provide an even faster way of selecting menu items. Pull down the **Fi**le menu again, as shown in figure 1.4. Notice the four menu items that have additional text on the right side of the menu list.

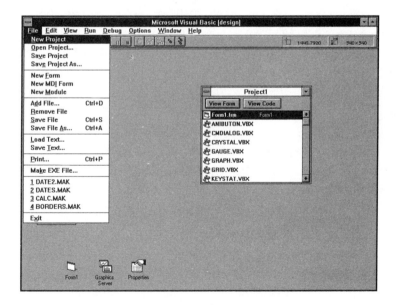

Fig. 1.4
The **F**ile menu.

For example, the **P**rint menu item has Ctrl+P next to it. This text represents the shortcut keystroke to access that menu item directly, without having to pull down the **F**ile menu and then select **P**rint. The plus sign (+) between the two keys signifies that the first key should be pressed and held while the second key is pressed.

Try to access the same menu item using each technique. First use the access keys to select **P**rint from the **F**ile menu. The Print dialog box appears. Then select the Cancel button to close the dialog box without taking any action. Now try the shortcut key. Without any menus pulled down, press and hold the Ctrl key and then press the P key. The Print dialog box appears immediately.

While some shortcut keys are assigned for compatibility with other Windows programs (such as Alt+F4 for **F**ile **E**xit), the rest are assigned based on frequency of use. The operations performed most frequently are assigned to *function keys*. These are the special keys across the top or on the left side of your keyboard; each one begins with the letter F, as in F1, F2, F3, and so on. Operations assigned to function keys are handy because they only require a single key press. You will appreciate this feature while you are getting started with Visual Basic. For example, the very first function key, F1, instantly invokes the on-line help.

Some menu items are executed immediately while others require more information. A menu item followed by ellipsis points (...) indicates that choosing the item will not execute the command immediately. You will either see another menu or a dialog box. You saw this earlier when you accessed the Print dialog box using **F**ile **P**rint.

While you are using Visual Basic, not all menu items are applicable at all times. When you can't use a menu item, it is *grayed.* Menu items normally appear as black text. When the text is gray you can still see the item, but you can't select it. Items are grayed rather than removed so you can remember menu item locations. If a menu item with an associated Toolbar button is grayed, the Toolbar button will also be grayed.

The Toolbar

The *Toolbar* is the row of picture buttons under the menu bar, as shown in figure 1.5. The icons on the face of the buttons represent the action taken when you press that button. For example, the button with an icon of an open file folder represents opening a project.

Fig. 1.5
The Toolbar.

Each Toolbar button represents a frequently performed action. Using these buttons makes performing actions faster and easier. Don't worry if you can't remember what each button does; there are menu items that perform the same operation as each Toolbar button.

There are five groups of buttons on the Toolbar. Use the first group to add new forms or modules—the basic building blocks of your projects. Use the second group to open or save a project. Use the next group to access the Menu Design dialog box and the Properties window (the Properties window is covered later in this chapter). Use the fourth group to start, pause, or stop the execution of your application while designing or debugging. And use the last Toolbar button group for debugging, which allows you to execute your application by stepping through it, set breakpoints, and view the values contained in variables. (These may sound like foreign terms right now, but you will find more information on debugging in Chapter 9.)

You may find that you don't use the Toolbar and would prefer the additional screen space for other purposes. You can hide the Toolbar by selecting **T**oolbar from the **V**iew menu. Notice that when the Toolbar is visible, a check mark appears to the left of the menu item, and when the Toolbar isn't visible, there is no check mark. This is Visual Basic's way of telling you whether the Toolbar is on or off.

The Project Window

Because each program you design will solve a different problem, each one will have different forms with different controls on them and different program code. Over time, it may become difficult to remember all the parts of your various designs. Again, Visual Basic provides a convenient solution—this time in the form of projects.

A *project* is a group of forms, code modules, and custom controls used by a particular Visual Basic program. In effect, a project and a program are synonymous. The pieces and parts of a program are displayed in the Project window, which is shown in figure 1.6.

As you work through the various projects described in this book, you will learn more about how the Project window helps you manage all the parts and pieces of your program.

Fig. 1.6
The Project
window.

> **Note**
>
> If you have code modules or forms that you would like to use in several projects, you can. You can add the same form, code module, or custom control to any number of projects. Just remember that any changes you make to a form in one project will appear on that form, in the other project, the next time the other project is opened.

The Toolbox

When you work in Visual Basic, you will see a collection of buttons at the left side of the screen, as shown in figure 1.7. This is called the *Toolbox*. The buttons in the Toolbox are called *controls,* and they represent objects you can place on your forms.

Fig. 1.7
The Toolbox.

If the Toolbox does not appear on your screen, you can display it by selecting the **T**oolbox menu item from the **W**indow menu. This menu option allows you to both hide and display the Toolbox.

The Visual Basic Toolbox contains two types of controls: regular and custom. The controls built into Visual Basic are *regular controls*. These are:

- Check box
- Combo box

- Command button

- Directory list box

- Drive list box

- File list box

- Frame

- Horizontal scroll bar

- Image control

- Label

- Line

- List box

- Option button

- Picture box

- Shape

- Text box

- Timer

- Vertical scroll bar

The remaining controls in the Toolbox (if any) are *custom controls*, which are not built into Visual Basic. Custom controls are added by including a special file, which contains the control, to your project. When you look at your Toolbox, custom controls don't appear any different than regular controls, and you use them the same way—by placing them on a form.

Removing and Adding Custom Controls. In the tradition of many other Windows programs, Visual Basic allows you to modify your environment extensively. One of the first actions you may want to take is to modify what controls are available in the Toolbox.

To reduce clutter in the Toolbox, as well as the time it takes to load your project, you may want to remove any unused controls. To remove a custom control, select the filename representing the control in the Project window. Then, from the **F**ile menu, select **R**emove File. The filename is removed from the Project window and the custom control is removed from the Toolbox.

Tip

If you don't know which Project window filename belongs to which custom control, you can use the Help system to discover the proper information. (The Help system is discussed later in this chapter.) Simply search for topics related to *custom controls,* and then display the only topic that is available— *Professional Edition Help Files*. This selection displays a list of all custom controls; if you choose one of these, you will learn the filename associated with the control.

To add a custom control to your project, select A**d**d File from the **F**ile menu. After you supply the filename for the control, it is added to the Project window and the appropriate button for the control appears in the Toolbox. By tradition, custom control files are kept in Windows' SYSTEM subdirectory; however, many third-party control providers create their own directories and store their custom control files there, when controls are installed.

Some custom control files contain more than one control. An example of this is THREED.VBX, a file which contains six custom controls: a 3-D frame, a 3-D option button, a 3-D check box, a 3-D command button, a 3-D panel, and a 3-D group push-button. If a file contains multiple controls, you cannot be picky about which controls in that file you want loaded—you can either load all of them or none of them; it is up to you.

Using Controls. The way you use a control is to place it on a form. There are two ways to do this: double-clicking and drawing. When you use the mouse to double-click the control in the Toolbox, VB places the control in the center of the form. You can then make changes to the control as necessary.

To draw the control, first select it by using the mouse to click on it in the Toolbox. (Make sure you don't double-click; that puts the control on the form as described in the previous paragraph.) Next, place your mouse pointer over the form on which you want to draw the control. Point to the position where you want a corner of the control placed. Now, click and hold the mouse button and drag the mouse. As you move the mouse, you see an outline that represents the size of the control you are drawing. When you release the mouse button, the control appears in the size you have drawn.

Notice that when you select a control that has already been placed on a form, eight *sizing handles* appear around the outside of the control. These handles look like little dots, as shown in figure 1.8.

Fig. 1.8
Sizing handles
on a control.

Sizing handles ——

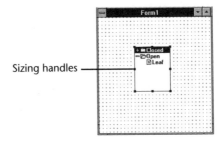

To change the size of a control, point to one of the sizing handles with the mouse, and then click and hold down the mouse button. When you do this, the mouse cursor changes to a double-headed arrow. As you move the mouse in one of the directions indicated by the arrow, the size of the control changes in that direction.

Basically, if you use one of the sizing handles on the sides of the control, you can move that particular side left, right, up, or down. If you use one of the sizing handles in the four corners, you can move the handle diagonally. This allows you to move two sides of the control at the same time. Remember that only the side (or sides) associated with the sizing handle is moved; all other sides retain their original position.

The Properties Window

Another major part of the Visual Basic environment is the *Properties window,* shown in figure 1.9. The purpose of this window is to list the properties of various controls you have placed in a form, as well as the properties of the form itself.

Fig. 1.9
The Properties window.

There is a reciprocal relationship between an object (either a form or controls in a form) and the information in the Properties window. The information in the window changes as you select different objects, or as you use the mouse to change an object. Conversely, you can modify the information in the Properties window, and your changes are automatically reflected in the object. The full purpose and meaning of the Properties window will become clearer after you work through Chapter 2.

Getting Help

Visual Basic comes with a complete on-line help system that you will find very useful as you learn to program. Earlier in this chapter, you learned a tip which indicated one particular way the Help system is useful (finding which filename is associated with which control). To access the Help system, you can do either of the following:

■ Select **H**elp from the main menu.

■ Indicate which item you need help with, and then press the F1 key.

When you choose **H**elp from the main menu, another menu appears that lists the different types of help you can receive. These options are very similar to help options for other Windows programs; if you are comfortable with using the help system in other programs, you will feel right at home here.

For example, if you choose the **C**ontents option from the **H**elp menu, you will see a "table of contents" for the Help system. From this table of contents, you can select the help topics that are the most appropriate to your needs. If you instead choose the **S**earch for Help On option, you can search for a particular help topic (searching for help is described later in this chapter).

The other way to access the Help system is to press the F1 key. The advantage of using this method over using the menu is that the F1 key is *context-sensitive*. This means that Visual Basic determines what you are currently doing, and then displays the help information that it believes is the most appropriate to your needs.

For example, if you are drawing a form and need assistance with a particular control, just select that control and press F1. Visual Basic jumps directly to the help information for that control. This method of accessing the Help system also works for different elements of the Visual Basic environment, such as the main menu, the Toolbar, the Project window, and the Toolbox. Just select the window with which you need help, and then press F1. Figure 1.10 shows an example of the Help screen displayed when you press F1 after selecting the Project window.

As another example, suppose you are editing program code (you will learn how to do this later) and you need help with a particular keyword. All you need to do is highlight the word and then press F1. Visual Basic shows you the help for that keyword.

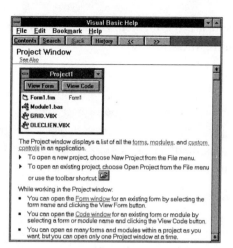

Fig. 1.10
An example Help
system window.

Searching for Help

One of the most powerful features of the Help system is the ability to search
for topics on which you need more information. This is done in either of two
ways:

■ Select the **S**earch for Help On option from the **H**elp menu.

■ Click the **S**earch button that appears at the top of any help window (see
figure 1.10).

Either method will result in the Search dialog box being displayed, as shown
in figure 1.11.

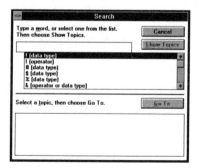

Fig. 1.11
The Search dialog
box.

Next type the specific word or phrase with which you need help. As you type,
the Help system displays a list of words and phrases that most closely match
what you are typing. When you see the word or phrase in which you are

interested, make sure it is highlighted. (This is done either by selecting it with the mouse or by using the arrow keys.)

Now you must display the topics related to your word or phrase. This display is made by either clicking the **S**how Topics button or by double-clicking the actual word or phrase. In the bottom portion of the Search dialog box, you will see a list of topics appear. These topics are related to the word or phrase you specified. Just highlight the desired topic and then click the **G**o To button. The Help system then displays the requested information.

Navigating the Help System

Take a look at a typical Help system window, as shown in figure 1.12. Notice that there are a group of buttons across the top of the window. You have already learned how to use one of these buttons (**S**earch). The other buttons allow you to navigate through the help file, reading information as you would in a book.

Fig. 1.12

The Help system navigation buttons.

The navigation —— buttons

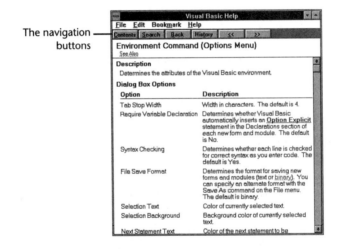

Tip

When you finish using the Help system, minimize the Help window instead of closing it. The next time you need help, Windows won't need to reload the Help system program, and you'll get help faster.

To move through the help file, you use the >> button to move forward and the << button to move backward. The His**t**ory button allows you to redisplay any of the help topics you previously viewed.

Visual Basic uses the standard Windows Help system to display information. To fully describe all the features of the Windows Help system would require an entire chapter in this book. It is a powerful tool that many Visual Basic users come to depend on heavily while writing their programs. If you have never used the Windows Help facility, you should take some time to explore it. When you need assistance, on-line help is usually the fastest way to get it. To become more familiar with the Windows Help system, choose the **H**ow to Use Help option from the **H**elp menu. (This is the **H**elp menu within the Help system, not the **H**elp menu within Visual Basic.)

Your Own Private Tutor

If you want to see a quick on-line tutorial of some Visual Basic features, choose **L**earning Microsoft Visual Basic from the **H**elp menu. The screen shown in figure 1.13 appears.

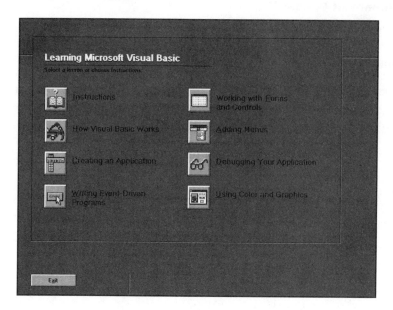

Fig. 1.13
Learning Microsoft Visual Basic.

Learning Microsoft Visual Basic is an interactive slide show that contains seven lessons concentrating on different themes in Visual Basic. It walks you through some Visual Basic features, with a graphical display of information. You can run Learning Microsoft Visual Basic at any time.

Learning by Example

Sometimes the best way to understand how something works is to look at an example. Microsoft provides quite a few good examples with Visual Basic. These examples are located in the SAMPLES subdirectory under the directory in which VB is installed (usually C:\VB). By opening an example project and examining its components, you not only get a different perspective on the Visual Basic programming process, but you also find some clever techniques for accomplishing common programming tasks.

Customizing Visual Basic

Given the same office, no two individuals will organize it the same way. John may like his desk by the window, and Jane may prefer hers facing the door. The Visual Basic programming environment is so advanced, it allows you to customize virtually any aspect of the environment. Some of the changes you make may apply only to your current project, while other changes will apply to all your projects.

Environment Options

Visual Basic uses a group of options, collectively referred to as *environment options,* to control how the VB program operates. These are called environment options because they control the Visual Basic environment.

To access these options, choose **E**nvironment from the **O**ptions menu. The Environment Options dialog box appears (shown in figure 1.14), which contains options that apply to all your projects.

Fig. 1.14

The Environment Options dialog box.

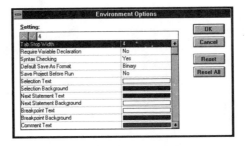

The first option you should change is Default Save As Format. Microsoft recommends setting this option to Text, which instructs Visual Basic to save your forms and code in a form that you can read and modify using any editor or word processor. The Binary option is only readable by Visual Basic.

The primary advantage of saving forms in the Text format is that if a file becomes corrupt (for whatever reason), you may be able to salvage it by editing the corrupt portion with a regular text editor. You also can print and modify the files directly by using an ASCII editor.

The advantages to saving files in Binary format don't outweigh the advantages of the Text format. By saving files in Binary format, your projects load slightly faster. This is because VB must first convert the files saved in Text format to Binary format (internally) before it can use them. In addition, project files stored in the Binary format consume somewhat less disk space than if they were stored in Text format. This may not be a real drawback, however, because all but the largest Visual Basic projects take relatively small amounts of disk space.

The second environmental option to change is Save Project Before Run. When this option is set to Yes, Visual Basic prompts you when you are about to run your project without saving the changes you've made. This helps to ensure that you don't lose any work if your program crashes as a result of the changes you've made.

Other environment options can be changed if desired, although these changes are not necessary at this point. Any changes you make to your environment are immediate; as soon as you close the Environment Options dialog box, the changes are made.

Project Options

Project options are those options which affect the application you're currently writing. To change the options for the current project, choose the **P**roject option from the **O**ptions menu. The Project Options dialog box appears, as shown in figure 1.15.

Fig. 1.15
The Project Options dialog box.

Of the three options presented in the Project Options dialog box, the one you are most likely to change is the Start Up Form option. Every program has a starting point, and your Visual Basic programs can start in only one of two places: with a form or with a procedure. Most of your programs will use a form as their starting point. This is why, when you start Visual Basic, you see a blank Form window on-screen. You can change which form is displayed when you start Visual Basic by changing the Start Up Form project option. The Start Up form can be any form in your project. Typically, the only time a procedure is used as the starting point is when there are no forms in your project.

The Command Line Argument option allows you to pass information into your Visual Basic program once you start running it. Your program can later retrieve this information with the Command function.

The last project option is Help File. Most Windows programs have an on-line help file similar to Visual Basic's. If you have a help file for your application, you can use the Help File option to identify it for Visual Basic. (You do not develop help files with Visual Basic; you use a separate help file compiler available from Microsoft. The process of developing help files is beyond the scope of this book.)

Your First Visual Basic Program

If a picture is worth a thousand words, then drawing a control on a form is worth at least a hundred lines of code. Controls allow you to add functionality to your applications with minimum effort. Earlier in this chapter you learned a little about what controls are and how to use them in a form you may be developing. Through the use of controls, you are about to see how quick and easy Visual Basic makes Windows programming.

For your first project you will make something simple yet useful—a calculator. The first step is to define what you want the project to accomplish. Because this is an introductory program, it will not offer a full range of calculating tools. Instead, it will focus on doing one thing—adding two numbers.

To accomplish this goal, your program must provide a way for the user to enter the numbers to be added, display the result of the addition, and a way to trigger the operation. All of these tasks are easily done with Visual Basic. Next you will take a look at how you go about implementing this type of a calculator.

Creating the Program

To begin your project, you will need to start with a clean slate. The best way to do this is to choose **N**ew Project from the **F**ile menu. Make sure that the Toolbar and the Toolbox are displayed, using the techniques covered earlier in this chapter.

After you have cleaned your slate, you are ready to create a real Visual Basic program. To begin, follow these steps:

- Place the controls necessary to define the user interface.

- Write the code necessary to produce the desired results.

This basic process is followed regardless of the type of Visual Basic program you are creating. These two steps are covered in the following sections.

Drawing the Interface

The interface for your calculator is defined in the Form window. When you start a new project, the Form window is completely empty. You will define the interface by placing controls within the form, as indicated earlier in the chapter. To create your calculator interface properly, you must follow these steps:

- Size the form to the approximate size for the program window.

- Define controls to hold two numbers, which will be added together.

- Define controls to display the result of the addition.

- Define a control that will trigger the addition.

Sizing the form is easy. Just use the mouse to size the window, as described earlier in the chapter. Make the Form window the size you want your calculator to be.

Now use the text box control, in the Toolbox, to create two text boxes. Figure 1.16 shows how these should be positioned in your Form window.

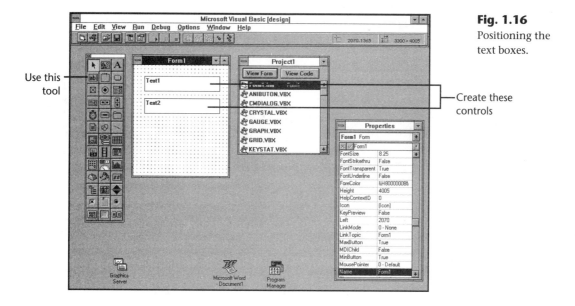

Fig. 1.16
Positioning the text boxes.

Next you can use the label control in the Toolbox to add a label to your form. This will be used to display the result of your addition. Figure 1.17 shows how this control should be positioned on the form.

Fig. 1.17
Positioning the
label control.

Use this
tool

Create this
control

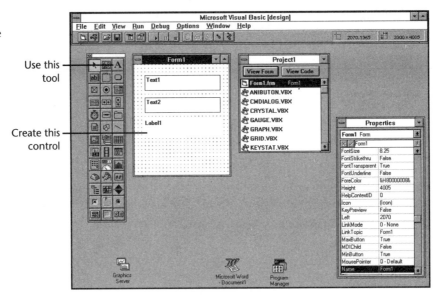

Finally, double-click the command button control in the Toolbox. You will recall from earlier in the chapter that when you double-click a control, it is placed in the center of the Form window. You then can use the mouse to move and resize the control so it is positioned properly, as shown in figure 1.18.

Fig. 1.18
Positioning the
command button.

Use this
tool

Create this
control

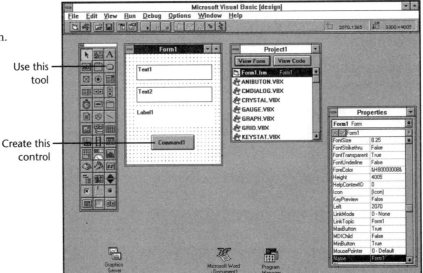

As a final step, you should change the text that appears on the command button control you just placed in your form. To do this, use the mouse to select the button, and then choose the Caption property in the Properties window. Notice that the value of this property is currently Command1, which is the default text on the button. If you change the value (you should change it to Add), the text on the command button also changes.

Caption and Name Properties

At the start of this chapter, you learned that Visual Basic is a programming language that allows you to work with screen objects while creating your programs. As you work with Visual Basic, you soon discover that there are all sorts of objects with which you work. These objects each possess different properties, which are defined through the use of the Properties window. Two of the properties with which you will become intimately familiar are the Caption and Name properties. While not used in all Visual Basic objects, these properties are used in quite a few of them.

The Caption property refers to the label used to identify the object to the user. For a form, this label appears in the title bar of the Form window. For other objects (such as command buttons), the label appears on the object itself. You can change the Caption property as you see fit.

The Name property is the name by which the object is known internally. This name is used in event procedures and can be used when developing your program code. Why would you want to change the Name property rather than use the default supplied by Visual Basic? Because as you develop larger and more complex programs, you will want to use object names that are meaningful in the context of what the object does. For small programs (such as this calculator project), you will probably never need to worry about changing the Name property.

The Caption and Name properties are discussed in more depth in Chapter 2.

Your user interface is now complete, and you are ready to write the program code.

Attaching Code. Many people refer to Visual Basic as an *event-driven* programming language. This reference is made because you typically program by defining what should happen when specific events occur. Examples of events are: clicking or double-clicking the mouse, or pressing a key on the keyboard.

Tip

While most Visual Basic programs may be designed using an event-driven approach, this is not the only way to program with the language. You also can design programs that accomplish a specific task that is not triggered by a particular event.

Throughout this book you will be introduced to many different types of events.

As indicated earlier, the calculator must add the two numbers contained in the text boxes and display the result in the label area. You want to perform the addition each time the command button is pressed. (You *press* a command button by clicking it with a mouse.) This action initiates a Click event to occur for the command button. If there is code in the command button's Click event procedure, that code will be executed whenever the event occurs.

The program code to be executed when a certain event happens is defined in the *Code window*. To access the Code window for the Click event, double-click the command button control in your form. The Code window appears, as shown in figure 1.19.

Fig. 1.19
The Code window.

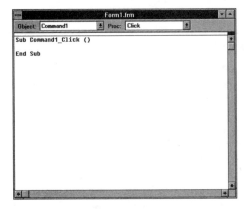

Notice the two selection boxes at the top of the Code window. The left one is used to indicate the object to which this procedure is being attached (in this case, to the command button), while the one on the right is used to indicate the event to which this code applies (in this case, to a mouse click). Because these settings are correct, you can start typing the procedure you want executed when the command button is clicked by the user.

Tip

Make the contents of the label control object equal to the contents of the first text box control object plus the contents of the second text box control object.

To add the values of the numbers in the two text boxes and store the result to the label, enter the following single line of code:

```
label1 = Val(text1) + Val(text2)
```

This program line may not make much sense to you, particularly if you have not programmed before. Basically, you are entering an equation. The part to the left of the equal sign (label1) indicates what value you are setting. In this case, `label1` is the name assigned by Visual Basic to the label control object placed in the form. Two other object names are used in this equation as well: `text1` and `text2`. These are the names of the two text box control objects placed in the form. In effect, this equation says the following, in plain English:

> *Make the contents of the label control object equal to the contents of the first text box control object plus the contents of the second text box control object.*

Don't be scared off by this formula; by the time you work through this book, you will be able to recite this type of equation in your sleep.

After you enter this line, close the Code window to keep it out of the way while you run the program. That is all there is to defining your program code!

Running Your Program

To run the calculator, select **S**tart from the **R**un menu. To add numbers and display the sum, type any numbers into the text boxes and click the command button. Figure 1.20 shows an example of what your final program may look like.

Fig. 1.20
The finished calculator.

The program you just created is not yet a true Windows program, however, because it can only be run from within the Visual Basic environment. You must complete one more step to turn it into a full-fledged Windows program.

Choose Ma**k**e EXE File from the **F**ile menu. You are then asked for a filename to use for the executable file. In this case, *CALC* would be a good name. Type **CALC,** and then press Enter or select the OK button. That's all there is to it! You just made your first independently executable Windows program using Visual Basic.

Saving Your Work

It is always a good idea to save your work often. In fact, you may save your work many times while you are working on a Visual Basic program. If you don't save your work, you will lose it whenever you exit Visual Basic or Windows.

You can save your project to your hard disk or a floppy disk at any time; just choose Save Project from the File menu. If this is the first time you have saved this project, you will be asked for a filename to use for your source code. (You would have achieved the same result by selecting the Save Project As menu option.) All you have to do is provide a module name. For example, you could use the name *CALC*. When you press Enter, the form module is saved under that name.

Next you are asked for the name to use for your .MAK project file. Traditionally, programmers call this a *make file*, although you know it as a project file. This file contains the information displayed in the Project window. You can use the same name as you did for the module file—CALC—and then press Enter.

Quitting Visual Basic

When your work is saved, you can exit Visual Basic the same way you would quit any other Windows program. The most common methods are as follows:

- Use the mouse to double-click the control-menu icon at the left end of the title bar.

- Choose the Exit option from the File menu.

Each method closes all the Visual Basic windows and returns you to the Program Manager.

Adding Your Program to a Group

Assuming that you created an executable .EXE program, you will probably want to test your calculator outside of the Visual Basic environment. You can assign your new program to an icon that appears in a program group. To do this, follow these steps:

- Choose **N**ew from the Program Manager's **F**ile menu. Make sure the Program **I**tem option is selected.

- Press Enter or click the OK button. You will then see the Program Item Properties dialog box, shown in figure 1.21.

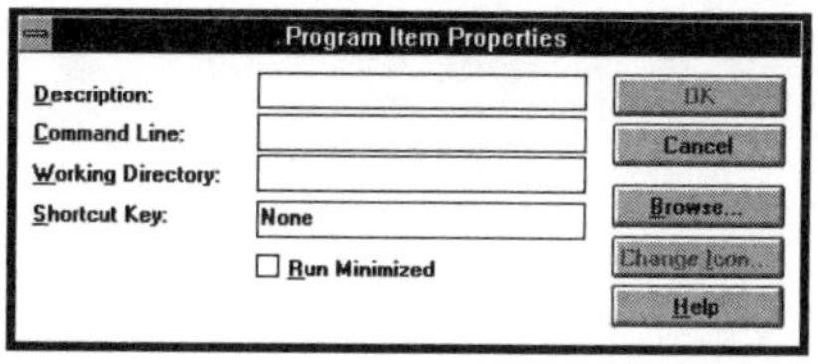

Fig. 1.21
The Program Item Properties dialog box.

- In the **C**ommand Line text box, type the name of the executable file you created, along with the full path name. In this case, you would use C:\VB\CALC.EXE.

- Press Enter or click the OK button. An icon titled Calc is added to your program group.

Now give your program a test drive! Start it as you do any true Windows program—by double-clicking the program icon. Your calculator should appear and function exactly as you created it.

From Here...

In this chapter, you learned how to use and customize the Visual Basic development environment. In particular, you explored:

- The menu bar, Toolbar, Toolbox, Project window, and Properties window.

- On-line and context-sensitive help.

- Customization of the Visual Basic development environment.

- Construction of a simple Visual Basic project.

- Making an executable Windows file from your project.

Chapter 2

Creating Forms

In Chapter 1, you learned a little about how you use forms. You also learned that forms are the basis of almost all Visual Basic programs, and you even used a form when you created a simple Visual Basic program. Although you can create a Visual Basic program without forms, you can't do it very often. All the examples in this book, therefore, will use forms.

In this chapter, you take a closer look at forms. You learn exactly how to use forms, from start to finish. Special emphasis is also given to object properties, with examples showing how they apply to forms.

Adding a New Form

Your Visual Basic programs can contain as many forms as you want. This makes sense because forms are nothing more than the windows used within a program. You add a new form to your project by choosing New Form from the File menu or by clicking the Toolbar's New Form button. The New Form button is the leftmost button on the Toolbar, and on its face is an icon of a form.

When you instruct Visual Basic to add a new form, a new Form window appears on-screen, and the default form caption appears in the title bar for the Form window. The default caption is always something like Form1, Form2, Form3, and so on. Each time you create a new form, the number at the end of the caption is incremented. Later in this chapter, you will learn how to change the default name and caption for a form.

Tip
Chapter 1 introduced you to object captions and names. Later in this chapter, you will learn more about these important concepts.

Changing Appearance and Behavior

It is safe to say that you will never use a form without altering its looks. You may want the form to be a different size or color. Or, perhaps you would like a thick border; maybe a thin one. Visual Basic provides many form properties you can choose from that can make your applications more functional, interesting, and enjoyable to use.

To change a form's properties, you use the Properties window, which was first discussed in Chapter 1 and now shown in figure 2.1. If the Properties window is not visible on your screen, you can display it by either pressing F4 or choosing Pr**o**perties from the **W**indows menu.

Fig. 2.1
The Properties window.

The Properties window displays a list of characteristics and specifications either for a form or for a control within a form. Because properties are only associated with forms and controls, the Pr**o**perties item on the **W**indow menu is not valid when you attempt to open the window, unless one of these objects (a form or a control) is selected. If the Pr**o**perties menu item is grayed, or if the F4 key has no effect, you must either select a form or a control before you can display the Properties window.

Down the left side of the Properties list box is the property name; down the right side is the current value of that property. You can browse through the list of properties the same way you would browse through any list box. Move one item at a time by using the keyboard's up- and down-arrow keys or by clicking the up or down pointing arrow on the scroll bar to the right of the list. Move a page at a time by pressing the Page Up and Page Down keys or by clicking the mouse on the scroll bar at the right side of the window.

Tip
If you forget the purpose of a particular property, or if you simply want to learn more about a property, select that property in the Properties window and press F1. This accesses the Visual Basic Help system, displaying context-sensitive help about the selected property.

Types of Properties

The properties you see listed in the Properties window are referred to as *design-time properties*. This simply means that you set their initial values while you are designing your project. There are other properties associated with forms which are not available from the Properties window. These are called *run-time properties* and can only be modified when a program is running. This modification is done through the use of programming commands rather than with a tool such as the Properties window.

One example of a run-time property is called `ActiveControl`. This property specifies the control on your form that has the *focus*—the control that is currently selected. Because `ActiveControl` only makes sense at run time, you won't find it listed in the Properties window.

Properties Related to Forms

The best way to understand the purpose of different properties is to take a look at what they do. The following sections introduce you to many of the properties related to forms. Remember that these are the properties you will most likely use as you get started with Visual Basic. These include:

- Color properties
- Text properties
- Size and location properties
- `BorderStyle`
- `Visible`
- The Control menu
- Picture properties
- `WindowState`

A few other properties will be introduced as well. Don't worry about the number of different properties that are available; many people are overwhelmed by the quantity and variety. Just because Visual Basic provides a property, it doesn't mean you have to change it. In fact, in most instances your form will be just fine if you use the default property values. As your experience grows, you will learn about the other properties. And, as your needs grow, you will come to appreciate the versatility offered by each of them.

Color Properties

Color is one of the most effective means of communicating; at the very least it is a way to add variety and spice to a program. For example, you may want to color code your forms as a way to indicate their purpose; you could use blue for a data-entry form and green for a report form. When you start placing controls on your forms, you will be able to modify the color of many of them as well. For example, if you use a control that displays a numeric value, you may want negative values to be displayed in red.

There are three different properties that control the color used in a form:

■ BackColor. This sets the background color used in a form.

■ ForeColor. This sets the foreground color used in a form.

■ FillColor. This is the color used by the VB application at run time to fill patterns in the background of a form.

In addition, if you are setting the color properties of a control, you can set the BorderColor property. This specifies the color used to display the border of certain controls.

Regardless of the color property you are setting, you use the same process. The value of a color property is always a number that represents the amount of each of the three primary colors (red, green, and blue) used to make up that color.

Fortunately, Visual Basic doesn't force you to use numbers to enter colors while designing. Double-click any of the color properties and you will see a palette of colors from which you may choose, as shown in figure 2.2. The palette contains 64 colors. The first 48 are predefined; the last 16 are definable by you.

Depending on the type of video board you have installed in your system, you may have over millions of different color combinations available. This doesn't mean your Visual Basic form's background can contain millions of different colors at the same time, however. Regardless of the number of colors your video card supports, Visual Basic generally allows you to only have up to

64 different colors on your form's background at the same time. The palette that defines these colors, however, can be composed of up to 64 colors drawn from as many colors as your hardware supports. Thus, if your video card is capable of displaying over 16 million colors, then the palette can consist of any 64 of those 16 million colors.

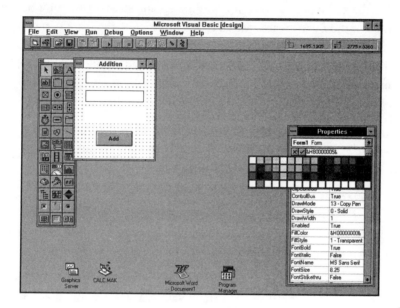

Fig. 2.2
Choosing a color from the palette.

To add your own colors to the Visual Basic palette, choose **C**olor Palette from the **W**indow menu. When the color palette is displayed (almost the same as what you saw in figure 2.2), click the Custom Colors >> button. Choose one of the 16 boxes in the bottom row and click Define Colors. The Define Color dialog box appears, as shown in figure 2.3.

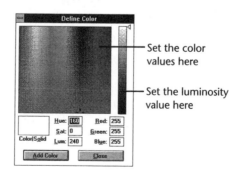

Fig. 2.3
The Define Color dialog box.

There are many different ways to represent colors. Visual Basic uses the same color coding schemes utilized by Windows. As you can see from the Define Color dialog box, you can set colors either through use of Hue, Saturation, and Luminosity settings, or by RGB (red, green, blue) values. The theory of color is a complex subject to which entire books are dedicated; it is definitely beyond the scope of this book. It is fortunate, indeed, that you don't need to know color theory to create custom colors in Visual Basic. Just use the mouse to click anywhere in the color selector (the large square of colors at the top of the dialog box) and the hue and saturation values automatically change. Use the mouse to click anywhere in the luminosity bar at the right side of the dialog box, and the luminosity value changes.

As you change the two pointers (color and luminosity), Visual Basic displays the selected color in the Color display box. When you see the color you want, click the **A**dd Color button to add it to the palette.

Text Properties

In Chapter 1 you learned how the Name and Caption properties relate to forms and objects. To fully understand these properties, you will need to know more about them.

When a new form is added to your project, its two text properties, Caption and Name, are automatically set to default values. You see these values in the top line of the selection box in the Properties window. Most Visual Basic programmers, however, change these defaults to reflect the proper title and purpose of the form.

Caption. Most Windows programs display some descriptive text in the title bar of the application's window. Sometimes this text is as simple as the name of the program. Most of the time, however, it will be the name you decide to assign to the dialog box being defined by your form. When you design programs with Visual Basic, you use the Caption property of the form to control the text displayed in the form's title bar.

To change a form's caption, double-click the Caption property in the Properties window. Then type the text you want to appear in the form's title bar. The text you type appears in the title bar immediately.

Name. If your application contains more than one form, you should find a way to refer to each form, besides the default name assigned by Visual Basic. This name is primarily used to refer to a form (from other program procedures) or to refer to controls within the form. For instance, if you change the name of a form from the default (such as Form1) to a descriptive name (such as GetRecord), you will have a much better idea of what the form is for when you refer to it from other parts of your program.

> **Note**
>
> A form's Name property does not refer to the filename in which the form is stored. You specify the filename in the File Save dialog box when you save the form module. The filename is not a property of the form; it is simply the name used by the operating system to reference the file in which the form is stored. The filename also appears in the .MAK project file.

By using descriptive names for your forms, you make it easier to remember the purpose of each form in your project. For example, the name DataEdit gives you a better idea about a form's purpose than the name Form4.

Size and Location Properties

Because forms represent program windows or dialog boxes that appear when your program is running, they must have a size and location which at least indicates where they appear and their dimensions on-screen. The size and location properties determine the form's dimensions and its whereabouts on-screen. These properties are:

- Height

- Left

- Top

- Width

Together these four properties define the location and size of a form. In the following sections, you will learn more about these properties.

Left **and** *Top*. The Left and Top properties specify the location of the form's left and top edges. In effect, these two properties define the location of the upper-left corner of the window. Although you can manually enter coordinates into the Properties window, it is much easier to simply drag the form with the mouse. As you move the Form window, the values of the Left and Top properties are automatically updated to reflect the new location.

Tip
Although there are several measurement scales available for dealing with a form's location and size, twips are the default. A *twip* is approximately 1/1440 of an inch. For more information on the use of measurement scales, refer to Que's *Using Visual Basic 3*. The examples in this book assume that the twip is used exclusively.

Height **and** *Width*. Visual Basic could have been designed with Right and Bottom properties in addition to Left and Top, but it wasn't. It makes more sense to specify the upper-left corner, and then specify the height and width of the window. This is what is accomplished through the use of the Height and Width properties. This way, the program itself may move the window by resetting Top and Left without accidentally altering its size.

Tip

If you need the location of the right side of the form, just add the value of Width to the Left property. For the bottom, add the value of Height to the Top property.

When combined with the Left property, Width determines where the right side of the form ends. Given the Top property, Height determines where the bottom of the form rests. As with the Top and Left, using the mouse to modify the height and width of the Form window is much easier than entering the values manually.

BorderStyle

Borders are used to define the boundaries of a window or a dialog box. Visual Basic allows you to specify the border type using the BorderStyle property. You can choose any of four different border types for your Form windows:

- None

- Fixed Single

- Sizable

- Fixed Double

The most common type of border is the Sizable border; thus, it is the default. If you choose BorderStyle, the user can change the size of the window when your program is running. Sometimes it is not appropriate for the window size to be changed, however. For example, if your form will be used as a dialog box, you will want to use a fixed border.

If you choose None as a BorderStyle, the window will not have a border; it will just end, without any demarcation between the window and the surrounding desktop. This may be fine if the form's BackColor (previous section) is a different color than the Windows desktop. If they are the same color, however, then your form will appear invisible. This gives the illusion of your controls lying on the desktop instead of in a window.

The Fixed Double border type is typically used when designing dialog boxes. If BorderStyle is used, the size of the window cannot be changed. (The user can still move the form, but the size remains the same.)

Finally, the Fixed Single border is primarily used to design windows (not dialog boxes) whose size you want to remain stable. Again, although the user can move the window, the window cannot be modified in size.

> **Note**
>
> Whenever you use the Fixed Single and Fixed Double border styles, the Minimize and Maximize buttons are not displayed on the form. These border styles do not, however, omit the Minimize and Maximize items from the window's control menu. To remove Minimize and Maximize from the control menu, set the MinButton and MaxButton properties to False.

The border style changes you make to your forms will not be immediately evident until you run your program. The reason for this is simple: if the border changed at design time and you selected a border type other than Sizable, you would have no way to resize the form at design time.

Visible

The form's Visible property determines whether the form is visible when it is loaded into the workspace of your program. The default value for this property is True, although you can also set it to False. (These are the only two settings.)

The Visible property allows you to indicate the initial condition of the window. While you are running the program, you can use other program instructions to change the property "on the fly." This is typically done when your application contains several forms, and you want to control the display of those forms as you switch from one to another. The screen doesn't become cluttered, and you can designate which form gets the attention of the user.

The Control Menu

In Windows, a control menu appears when you click the control-menu box, which is at the left end of a window's title bar (see figure 2.4). Visual Basic allows you to designate whether the menu appears at all.

Earlier in this chapter, you learned that you can use the MinButton and MaxButton properties to indicate whether the Minimize and Maximize menu items appear on the control menu; these properties should be used if you are designing a window whose size you don't want changed. Setting these properties to False means the menu items won't be displayed.

Fig. 2.4
The control-menu box.

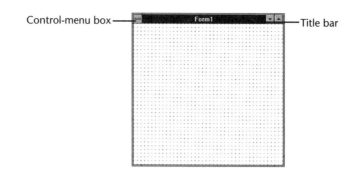

Control-menu box———Form1———Title bar

The ControlBox property is used to turn the control menu off entirely. If this property is set to False, then the control-menu box will not even appear on the window. A False setting should be used only when you are designing dialog boxes instead of windows.

Picture Properties

Pictures add pizzazz to your form, and Windows provides an excellent environment for working with graphics. Visual Basic gives you the tools to add graphics to your form through the use of two properties. The Icon property allows you to change which icon is used for a form, and the Picture property provides a method of adding pictures to your forms.

Icon. The Icon property determines which icon is displayed when the form is minimized. Although the default icon for Visual Basic forms is not very attractive, you can assign any icon you want. Figure 2.5 shows a simple example of the difference between the stock Visual Basic form icon and a custom icon.

Quite a few icons are provided with Visual Basic in the VB\ICONS subdirectory. They are all shown in Appendix B of the *Programmer's Reference* (provided with the Visual Basic software package).

Picture. You can place an image directly on the form itself using the Picture property. This is similar to using wallpaper in the Windows environment. The image is placed as a background in the window defined by the form, beginning at the upper-left corner. Figure 2.6 shows an example of a picture placed in a form.

There are four picture types recognized by Visual Basic. Table 2.1 shows their names and file extensions.

Tip
You can use the Icon Works application (found in the ICONWRKS subdirectory of the Visual Basic SAMPLES directory) to create new icons or modify existing ones. Use of this program is beyond the scope of this book, but it is a fun program with which to experiment.

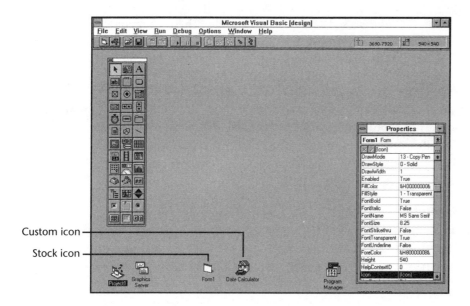

Custom icon

Stock icon

Fig. 2.5
Examples of stock and custom icons.

Tip
Visual Basic believes that there is a difference between a form icon and a program icon. The *form icon* is displayed when the window defined by the form is minimized. A *program icon* is displayed when the program resides in a group in Program Manager, waiting to be executed. You set the form icon using the Icon property; you set the program icon when you make an executable program file, as discussed in Chapter 1.

Table 2.1 Picture File Formats

Format	Extension
Bitmap	.BMP
Device Independent Bitmap	.DIB
Windows Metafile	.WMF
Icon	.ICO

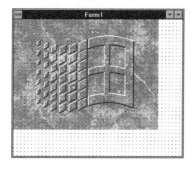

Fig. 2.6
An example of using a picture in a form.

Bitmaps represent a picture by storing the value of each pixel in that picture. The larger the picture being stored, the larger the size of the .BMP or .DIB file representing it. Bitmap files don't scale well. If you plan on stretching or shrinking the size of the picture, consider using a metafile.

An *icon,* or .ICO file, is a special type of bitmap file. These are graphic images that are limited to 32 pixels wide by 32 pixels high, and they are used solely as screen icons, for minimizing a window.

Metafiles represent a picture by depicting the way it is drawn. A metafile essentially says "Draw a line from point A to point B. Draw a circle centered at the point with coordinates X,Y with a diameter of Z." The .WMF format offers two advantages over bitmaps. First, it is usually more efficient with regard to storage space. Second, metafiles are not as distorted by changing their size from the size of the original picture.

Tip
Remember that the WindowState property sets only the initial window condition. You can change the condition while the program is running (using programming commands), or the user can change the condition by minimizing, maximizing, or restoring the window size.

WindowState

A form in Microsoft Windows can appear in only one of three states: maximized (consuming the entire screen), minimized (as an icon at the bottom of the screen), or normal (consuming a portion of the screen). The WindowState property determines whether the form is shown maximized, minimized, or normal.

Other Properties

Forms have quite a few additional properties. You can learn more about these properties by clicking the property in the Properties window and pressing F1 for context-sensitive help. For an in-depth look at utilizing additional properties, refer to Que's *Using Visual Basic 3*.

Revisiting the Calculator

Now that you know more about forms and how you can use properties to control them, it is time to put the information to work. The best way to do this is to look again at the Visual Basic project started in Chapter 1. Pull up the calculator and change some of the form and control properties to make it more professional.

Tip
When you open the file, you may only see the Project window; the Form window may be closed. If this is the case, click the View Form button at the top of the Project window.

Opening the Project

Before you can make changes to your calculator program, you must load it from disk either by clicking the Open icon on the Toolbar (third icon from the left) or by choosing **O**pen Project from the **F**ile menu. You will then see a dialog box where you can specify the project to open.

You may remember from Chapter 1 that the project name was *CALC.* Thus, you should open the file CALC.MAK. Everything will then be back to the same condition it was when you last saved your project.

Making Changes to the Form

Applying the information learned in this chapter, you may decide to make the following changes:

- Modify the caption shown on the title bar of the calculator.

- Change the form's border so the window cannot be resized by the user.

- Change the program's icon to something representative of your calculator.

- Modify the default information shown in the text boxes and label.

The easiest way to perform the first task is to select the form (use the mouse to click the Form window title bar) and then change the Caption property. Replace the default form caption (Form1) with a more descriptive name (such as Addition). Notice that as you type the new caption, it appears right away in the Form window title bar.

Next change the BorderStyle property to type 3-Double Fixed. You will not see any difference in how the Form window looks, but the window will behave differently after the program is executed.

Now change the Icon property. If you double-click the property, you can choose the icon file you want to use. After referring to Appendix B in the *Programmer's Reference* that came with Visual Basic, you may decide to use the MISC18 icon, which is a plus (+) sign. (This seems appropriate because the calculator will only perform addition.) Specify the icon file to use as VB\ICONS\MISC\MISC18.ICO, and then press Enter.

The final task involves picking a different object than the form itself. Use the mouse to select one of the text box controls in the form. Then change the Text property so it is empty (the default is the same as what you see in the control in the Form window). You should do this for both of the text box controls.

To make the same change in the label control, select it and then modify the Caption property. Delete the default value (Label1) so that nothing appears in the label.

After making these changes, you are ready to execute the program.

Tip

If you want, you can select the file containing your program's icon by clicking on different folders to get to your destination and selecting the proper file. In many cases, this is much quicker than entering a long path name for the icon file.

Testing the Result

In Chapter 1, you learned how to make an executable file from a Visual Basic program. You should perform the following steps:

1. Save your Visual Basic project.

2. Choose the Make EXE File option from the File menu.

3. Accept the default name for the file being created. (It is the same filename you used in Chapter 1, CALC.EXE.)

4. Press Enter.

Tip
If you don't see the new icon on-screen, select the icon and choose the **P**roperties option from the Program Manager's **F**ile menu. After you click the OK button, the icon is updated.

You can now exit Visual Basic and test your results. If you go to the program group you used at the end of Chapter 1 (the one where the icon for CALC.EXE is located), you should notice that the icon now reflects the new icon for the program. The icon was changed automatically when you made the .EXE file.

Double-click the icon and you should see your improved calculator on-screen, as shown in figure 2.7. Notice there are no default values in the calculator, and you cannot resize the calculator window, all of which is in line with what you wanted in the first place.

Fig. 2.7
The improved
calculator.

From Here...

In this chapter, you learned about the properties of forms and how to do the following:

■ Add new forms to your project.

■ Change the appearance and behavior of forms (and controls).

■ Change the colors associated with a form.

■ Change the text properties used by a form.

■ Modify the initial location and size of a form.

■ Change the type of border used by a form.

■ Control whether a form is displayed when your Visual Basic program is executed.

■ Change how your form displays (or doesn't display) a control menu.

■ Assign an icon to your form.

■ Use a graphic image as a picture within a form.

■ Set the initial state of the window to either maximized, minimized, or normal.

Chapter 3

Adding Functionality

To make your programs useful, they must do more than just display a form. The majority of this chapter takes you on a guided tour of the Visual Basic Toolbox. The Toolbox contains the standard Windows interface elements, which in Visual Basic are called *controls*. When you place these controls on a form, they provide a way for your program to accept input and display results. If forms are the foundation of your programs, then controls are the plumbing and wiring—they handle most of the routine activity.

In addition to learning about controls, you will learn how to effectively use the controls and how to manipulate the properties associated with the controls. By the time you reach the end of this chapter, you will be able to apply this information to create professional-looking programs, at least as far as the user interface is concerned.

Your Toolbox

In Chapter 1, you learned about the Toolbox, which is the repository of all the controls you can use in your Visual Basic programs. The Toolbox does not need to be displayed when you are programming in Visual Basic, but it is helpful when you are designing your forms. To display Visual Basic's Toolbox, choose **T**oolbox from the **W**indow menu.

After the Toolbox is displayed, you can start using it to add controls to your forms. Adding controls to your projects is a three-step process:

1. Add the required controls to the form.

2. Set the properties of the controls.

3. Attach any necessary code to the controls' event procedures.

Each step is important to the development of your programs, but the first two can be particularly time-consuming, especially if your program does quite a bit of user interaction. The first step is done exclusively with the Toolbox, so you will learn much about it in this chapter. The second step can be done either with the Properties window or under program control; the basics for this step will also be covered in this chapter. The final step involves actually creating programming code, and is best deferred to later chapters.

The easiest way to understand how to do these steps (at least the first two) is to get a firm grasp on the different controls you have available. After you know what the controls are, you can pick the right one for the right job, and then set the properties of that control. In the next several sections, you will learn about different types of controls made available by Visual Basic.

Working with Controls

In Chapters 1 and 2, you learned how to start working with controls. For example, you learned that you can place a control in a form by either of these methods:

- **Placing the control.** In the Toolbox, double-click the tool that represents the control you want to place in your form. This places the control in the center of the form.

- **Drawing the control.** In the Toolbox, click the tool that represents the control you want to use in your form. This selects the tool. Then use the mouse to draw the control in the form. You first use the mouse to point to where you want a corner of the control, and then click and hold down the mouse button. Move the mouse and release the button when the control is the desired size.

There are other techniques you can use when working with controls, however. These include the following:

- Changing properties

- Copying controls

- Deleting controls

- Moving controls

- Resizing controls

As you work with controls in your forms, you will use these techniques over and over again. This is particularly true because controls tend to be the building blocks of Visual Basic programs.

Before you can take any action with regards to a control, you must first select it. To select a control, point to it within your form and then click it once with your mouse button. The following sections introduce you to the ways you can manipulate controls.

Changing Control Properties

As you worked through Chapter 2, you learned about forms and their properties. Properties also apply to controls. Each control you can use within Visual Basic can have dozens of properties associated with it. These properties are listed in the Properties window, and they will differ (to some degree) based on the type of control you are using.

Many of the properties associated with controls are very intuitive in nature. You can change them and the behavior or appearance of the control will change accordingly. As you work through the examples in this book, you will learn more about the individual properties of many controls.

It would be virtually impossible, however, to list every possible property for every possible control—the possible combinations could number well into the thousands. Thus, it is far more valuable for you to learn how to discover more about properties on your own. That way, if you run across a property that is not described in this book, you can still get information about what it does.

The best way to get information about a property is to follow these steps:

1. Select the object (form or control) whose properties you want to change or learn more about.

2. In the Properties window, select the property in question.

3. Press the F1 key, which results in Visual Basic displaying context-sensitive help about the property.

Later in this chapter, you will learn about some of the more common control properties and how to use them.

Run-Time Changes. You already know from Chapter 2 that you can set properties when you design a form and then change them as your program

Tip
If you need help on the techniques for changing properties, refer to Chapters 1 and 2. All the information provided in this chapter assumes you already know how to change properties.

is running. The same is true for controls—basically you set the initial property values, and then these can be changed when your program is running.

To alter a particular property of a control while your program is running, your program instructions must use the following format:

```
[form.]control.property = value
```

Make sure that what you substitute for `form` and `control` correspond to the `Name` property assigned to the form and control whose property you are changing. (Using the `form` specification is only necessary if the program code is referring to a control attached to a different form than the one currently selected.)

For example, consider the `Enabled` property (detailed later in this chapter). When you are first designing your program, you can initially set whether the control is enabled or disabled. You may want this state to be changed as your program is running, however. If you want to change the `Enabled` property of a control named `Command1` in a form named `Form2`, you could use the following program line:

```
Form2.Command1.Enabled = False
```

Control Values. As you will learn after using Visual Basic for a while, each control has a primary purpose. For example, the primary purpose of a label control is to display short amounts of information. For text boxes, the primary purpose is to display or accept larger amounts of text.

Visual Basic refers to the property most closely associated with the control's primary purpose as the control's *value*. The benefit of knowing this is that when your program is running, your program can change the value of the control without needing to explicitly indicate which property you are changing. For example, these two lines of code perform exactly the same action because the `Caption` property is the `Label1` control's value:

```
Label1.Caption = "Last Name"
Label1 = "Last Name"
```

In addition to saving some typing, using a control's value is slightly faster. Table 3.1 lists some Visual Basic controls and their default properties.

Table 3.1 Controls and Their Values

Control	Value
Check box	Value
Frame	Caption
Label	Caption
Option button	Value
Text box	Text
Timer	Enabled

Moving Controls

You move a control the same way you move other objects in Windows. After you have selected the control, use the mouse to point to the object. Then click and hold down the mouse button. As you move the mouse, the control also moves. When you release the mouse button, the control is "dropped" at that location.

Resizing Controls

To resize a control, you must use the handles that appear around it when the control is selected. (This procedure was also covered in Chapter 1.) There are eight of these sizing handles, each appearing as a small dot or a small square (see figure 3.1).

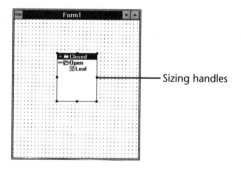

Sizing handles

Fig. 3.1
Sizing handles
on a control.

To change the size of the control, point to one of the sizing handles with the mouse, and then click and hold down the mouse button. When you do this, the mouse cursor changes to a double-headed arrow. As you move the mouse in one of the directions indicated by the arrow, the size of the control changes in that direction.

Copying Controls

When you have one control on a form, you can add additional controls of the same type by copying the existing control to the Clipboard and pasting as many copies as you need. One advantage this technique offers is that the copies will have properties identical to those of the source control. If you need several controls with identical properties, set the properties of the source control before copying it to the Clipboard.

To copy a control after it has been selected, choose **C**opy from the **E**dit menu, or press Ctrl+C. The control and its properties are then copied to the Clipboard. Choose **P**aste from the **E**dit menu, or press Ctrl+V. A dialog box appears, as shown in figure 3.2.

Fig. 3.2
A Visual Basic
warning.

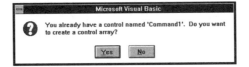

Visual Basic is warning you that you already have a control on your form with a particular name (in this case, Command1). This warning occurs because the Name property is copied to the Clipboard along with all the other properties. Because you only want to make another copy of this control, click the **N**o button.

> ### Note
>
> A *control array* enables several controls of the same type to share a single name, and therefore a section of code. Control arrays also provide a mechanism for adding and deleting controls at run time. (For example, to have the program generate six or seven buttons of a given type.) Control arrays are an advanced topic that is beyond the scope of this book, but you can find a complete discussion of them in Que's *Using Visual Basic 3*.

After the copy of the control is pasted in your form, all its properties are identical to the original control with one exception—the Name. The Name property has been changed by Visual Basic to include the next available numeral for this particular type of control. This change is because no two controls of the same type can have the same name, unless they are part of a control array.

> **Note**
>
> Notice that only the Name property is changed; the Caption property is not. This can be confusing to new Visual Basic programmers, so it is important that you must understand the difference between the Name and Caption properties. If you need a refresher, refer back to Chapter 1.

Deleting Controls

Deleting controls from a form is perhaps the easiest way to manipulate them. Just select the control you want to delete and then press the Delete key. The control is removed from the form.

Just be sure to modify any program code that may have referred to the control. If you don't, you could get errors when you later try to run the software.

Commonly Used Controls

You can use many different controls in your Visual Basic programs. In fact, if you look at the Toolbox, you will notice that it includes 39 different tools, of which 38 allow you to create controls in your forms. Obviously not all of these controls will be used in your programs; in fact, in most of your programs you will only use a handful of these controls.

The following sections introduce you to the most commonly used controls. A couple of these controls will already seem familiar—you used them in earlier chapters when you were developing the calculator program.

> **Note**
>
> Not all the controls available in the Toolbox will be covered in this chapter—only the most common ones. If you need detailed information on all the Visual Basic controls, refer to Que's *Using Visual Basic 3*.

Command Buttons

Command button controls are, perhaps, the most frequently used in a Windows program. They have a 3-D look that invites the user to press them. When pressed, they appear to move in and then back out, like a push-button on a piece of electronic equipment.

In the Toolbox, the command button control is represented by a rectangle with rounded corners and a shadow. You can use the techniques described in Chapter 1 to place a command button control in your form. For an indication of which tool to use and what you are creating, see figure 3.3.

Fig. 3.3

The command button control.

This button ⎯⎯

creates this control

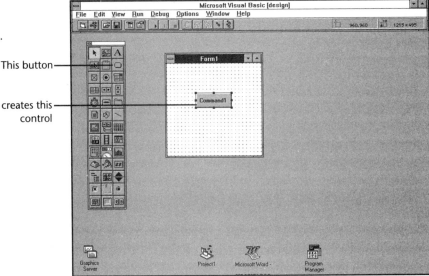

The first command button control placed on your form has the word Command1 on its face; this is a default caption. The second command button control's caption is Command2; the third is Command3, and so on. To change the caption, change the value assigned to the Caption property for the command button control.

Labels

Visual Basic's label control is named appropriately. Use a *label* wherever you must provide a description of another control—for example, above a text box or near a group of option buttons.

You can also display brief text with labels. A simple answer such as *Yes* or *No*, or the result of a numerical calculation, is easy to display using a label. That is why a label control was used in the calculator program example in Chapter 1 and Chapter 2.

In the Toolbox, the label control is represented by a large capital letter *A*. You can use the techniques described in Chapter 1 to place a label control in your form. For an indication of which tool to use and what you are creating, see figure 3.4.

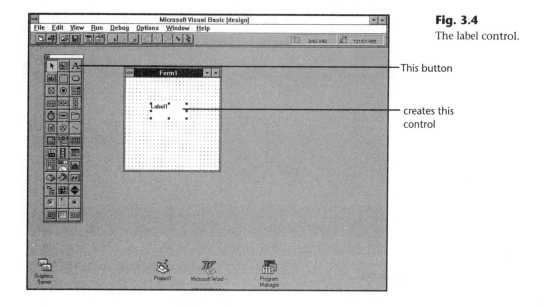

Fig. 3.4
The label control.

This button

creates this control

The first label control placed on your form contains the word Label1; this is a default caption. The second label control's caption is Label2; the third is Label3, and so on. To change the caption, change the value assigned to the Caption property for the label control.

Text Boxes

When you want to display a lot of text, and you want the user to be able to change that text or enter their own text, you should use a text box control instead of a label control. Text boxes can hold up to 32,000 characters and offer additional features for dealing with a larger quantity of text. For example, users can cut, copy, and paste text in a text box.

In the Toolbox, the text box control is represented by the lowercase letters *ab* within a rectangle. You can use the techniques described in Chapter 1 to place a text box control in your form, although drawing the text box is generally the best approach. For an indication of which tool to use and what you are creating, see figure 3.5.

The first text box control placed on your form contains the word Text1, the second contains Text2, the third contains Text3, and so on. To change this text, change the value assigned to the Text property for the text box control.

Fig. 3.5
The text box
control.

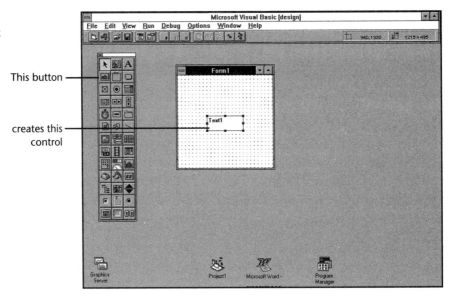

This button ——

creates this ——
control

Check Boxes

Sometimes you only need a *Yes* or *No* answer. Check box controls are perfect for collecting simple input such as *Yes* or *No*, *True* or *False*, or *On* or *Off*. Check boxes are used in many different Windows programs. They consist of a small square that you can turn on or off; when the square is selected, an *X* appears in it.

In the Toolbox, the check box control is represented by a square with an *X* in it. You can use the techniques described in Chapter 1 to place a check box control in your form. For an indication of which tool to use and what you are creating, see figure 3.6.

Tip
When your program is running, only one option button at a time in any grouping can be selected. Groupings are either the entire form or are defined by a frame control or a picture control. See the sections on frame and picture controls for more information.

The first check box control placed on your form contains the word Check1; this is a default caption. The second check box control's caption is Check2; the third is Check3, and so on. To change the caption, change the value assigned to the Caption property for the check box control.

Option Buttons

The option button is a cousin of the check box. Option buttons permit the selection of one option from several alternatives. While the use of a single check box may make sense, option buttons always appear in groups of two or more. When your program is running, clicking one of the option buttons automatically turns the others off. This is why option buttons are sometimes referred to as being *mutually exclusive*—only one of them can be selected at a time.

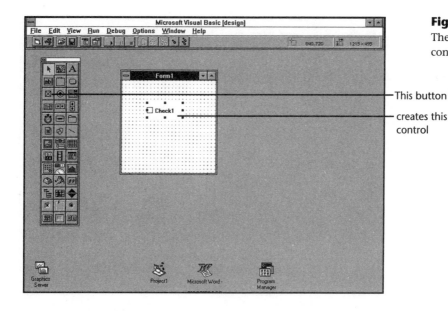

This button

creates this control

In the Toolbox, the option button control is represented by a circle with a dot in it. You can use the techniques described in Chapter 1 to place an option button control in your form. For an indication of which tool to use and what you are creating, see figure 3.7. (Note, however, that you will typically be creating an entire group of option buttons, rather than the single one shown in this figure.)

The first option button control placed on your form contains the word Option1; this is a default caption. The second check box control's caption is Option2; the third is Option3, and so on. To change the caption, change the value assigned to the Caption property for the option button control.

Grouping Controls

There will come a time when your forms get complex enough that you must categorize different controls in the form. The most common example of this is when you must group option button controls. The control you use to perform these groupings is the frame control.

In the Toolbox, the frame control is represented by a rectangle with letters *xyz* at the top of the rectangle. You can use the techniques described in

Tip

If you are going to group controls using the frame control, be sure to place the frame in your form prior to placing any of the contents of the frame. If you don't (for example, if you move the controls into the frame later), Visual Basic will not recognize the fact that the controls are grouped within the frame.

Chapter 1 to place a frame control in your form. For an indication of which tool to use and what you are creating, see figure 3.8.

Fig. 3.7
The option button control.

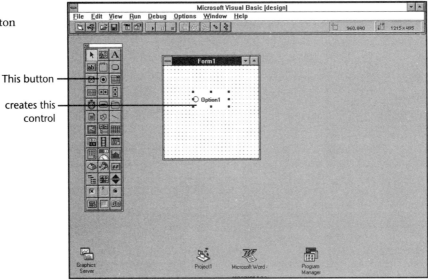

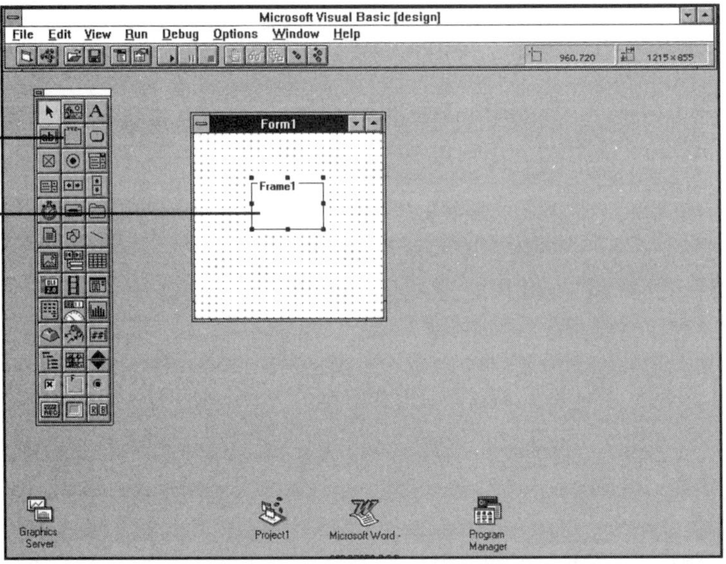

This button —

creates this — control

Fig. 3.8
The frame control.

This button —

creates this — control

The first frame control placed on your form contains the word Frame1; this is the default caption. The second frame control is Frame2, the third is Frame3, and so on. To change the caption, change the value assigned to the Caption property for the frame control.

Scroll Bars

For some user interfaces, you may want to use scroll bars for user input. For example, you may want the user to be able to set a volume level, brightness, or color intensity. Visual Basic provides two different scroll bar controls you can use—one horizontal and the other vertical.

In the Toolbox, the horizontal scroll bar control looks just like a horizontal scroll bar. You can use the techniques described in Chapter 1 to place the scroll bar control in your form. For an indication of which tool to use and what you are creating, see figure 3.9.

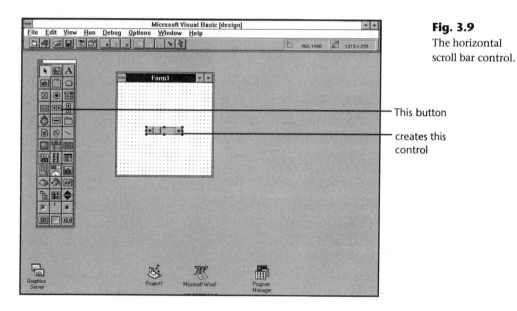

Fig. 3.9
The horizontal scroll bar control.

This button —

creates this control —

The first horizontal scroll bar control placed on your form is named HScroll1; this is the default Name property. The second horizontal scroll bar control is HScroll2, the third is HScroll3, and so on.

The vertical scroll bar control, in the Toolbox, looks just like a vertical scroll bar. You can use the techniques described in Chapter 1 to place the scroll bar control in your form. For an indication of which tool to use and what you are creating, see figure 3.10.

Fig. 3.10
The vertical scroll
bar control.

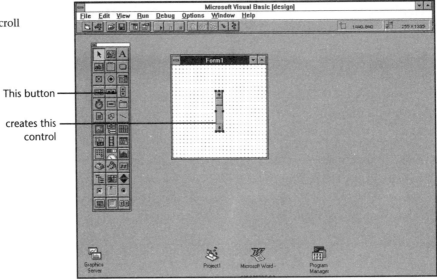

This button ——

creates this ——
control

Tip
You can change
the length or
width of a scroll
bar the same way
you would resize
any control. You
get the most satis-
factory results,
however, if you
only change the
width of the hori-
zontal scroll bars
and the height of
the vertical scroll
bars. This is be-
cause the arrows at
the end of the
scroll bars are
proportioned
correctly for only a
certain height and
width. Play with
the sizing to make
sure you get the
satisfactory results
you want.

The first vertical scroll bar control placed on your form is named VScroll1;
this is the default Name property. The second vertical scroll bar control is
VScroll2, the third is VScroll3, and so on.

Listing Information
Sometimes there are so many available options that to list them all would
take up too much space. On these occasions you will find two different controls very helpful. The list box control is used for simple lists, while the
combo box control is much more versatile. Each has its own purpose, however.

List Boxes. List boxes can hold thousands of items, yet consume only a few
lines on-screen. A list box is like a window through which you view information a little at a time. For example, if you are using Visual Basic to develop a
mailing list management program, you might use a list box to provide the
user with a list of possible countries that can be specified for a particular
address.

In the Toolbox, the list box control is represented by a small rectangle with
lines and arrows in it. You can use the techniques described in Chapter 1 to
place a list box control in your form. For an indication of which tool to use
and what you are creating, see figure 3.11.

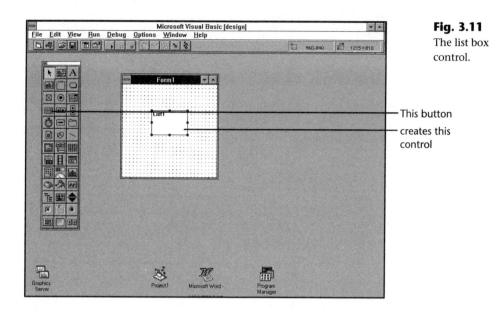

Fig. 3.11
The list box
control.

The first list box control placed on your form contains the word List1, the second list box control is List2, the third is List3, and so on. These only represent the Name property; the name will not appear when your program is executed. If you need a label for your list, you will need to use a label control.

Combo Boxes. The combo box got its name from the fact that it combines two other controls: the text box and the list box. Visual Basic allows you to create three different combo box styles:

- Dropdown Combo

- Simple Combo

- Dropdown List

You specify which style you want by changing the Style property for your combo box.

The Dropdown Combo style conserves space on your forms. It normally appears as a text box with an arrow next to it. When your program is running and you click the arrow, a list box drops down from the text box, permitting selection from the list. You can either select a choice from the list or type your choice into the text box.

The Simple Combo style does not utilize a pull-down list. Instead, it appears as a text box with a list permanently displayed beneath it. Like the Dropdown Combo style, you can either select from the list or type into the text box. The number of items visible in the list is determined by the Height property.

A Dropdown List style looks and behaves like a Dropdown Combo style, but it doesn't allow you to enter text—you must choose from the list.

In the Toolbox, the combo box control looks much like the list box control, except it shows a text box above the list. You can use the techniques described in Chapter 1 to place a combo box control in your form. For an indication of which tool to use and what you are creating, see figure 3.12.

Fig. 3.12
The combo box control.

This button creates this control

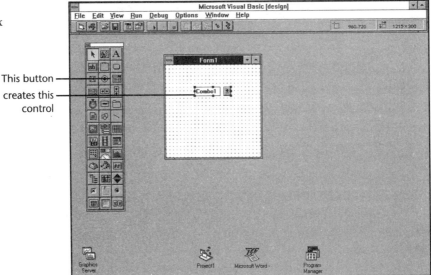

The first combo box control placed on your form contains the word Combo1, the second combo box control is Combo2; the third is Combo3, and so on. To change the text, change the value assigned to the Text property for the combo box control.

Managing Lists. It stands to reason that if you can present a list of information in either a list box or a combo box, there must be a way to manipulate the information in the list. Visual Basic allows you to do this through the use of methods.

Methods are just a way of acting on a control—as in manipulating what appears in a list. Methods are used entirely under program control through the use of program code.

When it comes to list boxes and combo boxes, there are three different methods you can use. These methods control how you add and remove items from a list.

The AddItem method is used to add items to a list. How those items subsequently appear in the list will depend on several of the properties you have set for the list box or combo box, particularly the Sorted property.

The *AddItem* Method

The format of AddItem is

```
[form.]control.AddItem item[, index]
```

Where index is the position in the list where item will be added.

Examples

```
List1.AddItem Text1.Text
AddRecord.List2.AddItem "Fifth Item", 5
```

The first example adds the text contained in text box Text1 at the end of the list. The second example adds the phrase Fifth Item to the list in the fifth position regardless of whether sorting is turned on or not. The list index starts at zero.

The RemoveItem method deletes an item in a list box or combo box list.

The *RemoveItem* Method

The format of RemoveItem is

```
[form.]control.RemoveItem index
```

Where index is the position of the item within the list. The list index starts at zero.

Example

```
Form3.List1.RemoveItem 4
```

This example removes the fourth item in the list.

The Clear method empties a list box or combo box of its contents. It is equivalent to repeatedly using the RemoveItem method until all the list items are removed.

The *Clear* Method
The format of Clear is

        [*form.*]*control*.Clear

Clear completely empties the list box regardless of the number of entries it contains.

Example

        List1.Clear

Control Properties

Earlier in this chapter, you learned how you can view, change, and work with properties. Many of these properties are intuitive, and a good number of them work the same way in relation to controls as they do in relation to forms (see Chapter 2).

Several properties are so common in their use that they deserve special treatment and discussion. In the following sections, you will learn about these properties and how their use can enhance your programs.

Caption

Captions are used as on-screen identifiers for many different types of controls. This property applies to command button, label, check box, option button, and frame controls.

Visual Basic also allows you to create hot keys for use with captions. Everyone has used Windows programs in which there are hot keys on command buttons or other controls. These hot keys are represented by an underlined letter, and indicate that you can select the control by pressing the Alt key in combination with the underlined letter.

You can create your own hot keys by using the ampersand (&) character when setting the Caption property. For example, suppose you wanted to set the caption for a command button to the word *Go,* and you wanted a hot key of Alt+G. To do this you would set the Caption property equal to &Go. The ampersand indicates that the following character (the G) is the hot key. Visual Basic takes care of the rest—when your program is running, the G will be underlined and the program will automatically recognize what to do when Alt+G is pressed.

Text

Earlier you learned about the Caption property, which is used to display small amounts of information to the user. Some controls (such as the text box and combo box controls) are used to display larger amounts of information. In these cases, text that is displayed by the control is assigned to the Text property.

All the information presented later in this chapter about fonts and text characteristics also applies when the value of the Text property is displayed.

Text Box Properties

There are a few properties that are unique to text boxes. These properties are used to control how information is displayed in the text box.

When you place a new text box on a form it will, by default, only show a single line of text—regardless of how tall you make the text box. You can still browse through the text using the arrow keys, but only the one line is displayed. To have Visual Basic display more than one line in a text box, set the MultiLine property to True.

Because text boxes allow a user to enter large amounts of text, you may have a need to limit their input. After all, why let the user input 200 characters if you only need 5? To limit the length of the input, set the MaxLength property to the desired length.

When MaxLength is set to zero (the default), the text box can hold any amount of text up to about 32,000˚characters. If you set MaxLength to any positive nonzero value, you limit the number of characters that can be entered to that value. After the limit is reached, your system will beep when more keys are pressed.

You may also find yourself using text boxes for getting passwords from the user. For example, the user may need to enter a password before he or she can access information in your program. This is where the PasswordChar property comes in. Normally, this property is not set; it is empty. If you change

PasswordChar to a character, that is the character displayed when the user starts typing. Thus, if you have set PasswordChar to the letter X, when the user types a five-character password, all the user will see is XXXXX in the text box. Internally, however, Visual Basic tracks exactly what was typed.

Appearance of Your Text

One of the strongest features of Windows is the attractive way in which it can present information. Visual Basic, through Windows, gives you complete control over how your text looks on-screen. If you are using a control that displays text, you can use Visual Basic to modify how that text is presented.

Understanding Fonts. The word font refers to the style of type (characters) used in the display of information. Each font has distinguishing characteristics such as the typeface, which refers to the general appearance of a character: the type style (such as italic or bold) and the type size (or how large the character appears). To change the appearance of text on your controls, Visual Basic provides several different properties.

Changing Fonts. By default, Visual Basic uses the MS Sans Serif font for all the controls you create. If you want to specify a different font, just change the FontName property.

Tip

When you are running your program, you can use the FontCount and Fonts properties of the Printer or Screen objects to determine all fonts available on that object. See Visual Basic's on-line help for more information on using the FontCount and Fonts properties.

The fonts available to Visual Basic depend on the fonts installed on your computer system. Visual Basic knows which fonts are installed; therefore, at design time, you can select from a list of available fonts. If you distribute your application to others, you must make sure they have the same fonts available on their system. If they don't, your program will not appear the same to them as it does to you. The simplest solution is to use the default MS Sans Serif font. This very readable font is available on all Windows 3.0 and Windows 3.1 systems.

With the introduction of Windows 3.1 came the inclusion of a new font technology called *TrueType*. TrueType fonts are constructed in such a way that they can be scaled without losing their good looks—in many ways they are a competitor to PostScript fonts. If your program requires using fonts of many different sizes, consider using TrueType fonts. (If you use the default MS Sans Serif font, you will not be using a TrueType font, unless your WIN.INI file substitutes it for Arial.)

You are not limited to using fonts supplied with Windows. There are, in fact, thousands of different fonts you can purchase from many different sources. If you choose to use a font from a third-party vendor, you should be aware of one thing—most vendors do not allow you to redistribute their fonts. They require each user to purchase a copy. If you intend to distribute your applications to others, be sure to take this into account when selecting the fonts you use.

Changing Other Text Properties. Besides specifying the type of font to use, you also can use Visual Basic to control how that font looks. Table 3.2 describes other properties which can be used to modify text used in your controls.

Table 3.2 Visual Basic Text Properties

Property	Value	Result
FontBold	True False	Text appears in bold Text appears normal
FontItalic	True False	Text appears in italics Text appears normal
FontSize	A number	The size of each text line in points. Each point is approximately 1/72 of an inch.
FontStrikethru	True False	Text appears with a line horizontally through the middle of it Text appears normal
FontTransparent	True False	Background shows through text Text blocks background
FontUnderline	True False	Text appears underlined Text appears normal

Alignment

If you have used a word processor for any length of time, you already know that there is more than one way to align text in a document. Although not quite as versatile as a word processor, Visual Basic also allows you to align the text within various controls. Primarily, this applies to any displayable text set with the Caption or Text properties.

The Alignment property is applicable to the label, text box, check box, and option button controls. Table 3.3 lists the various Alignment property settings you can use. You should note, however, that not all of these settings are available for all controls. For example, you cannot center-align check boxes and option buttons.

Table 3.3 Visual Basic alignment options	
Alignment	**Meaning**
Left Justify	Align the text at the left side of the control.
Right Justify	Align the text at the right side of the control.
Center	Center the text within the control.

Value

You already know that controls such as check boxes and option buttons can be either on or off, true or false. The Value property allows you to indicate the initial setting for the control. If you set the Value property to either 1 or True (depending on the control), then the control is shown on the form as selected.

> **Note**
>
> Remember that only one option button in any grouping can be selected. Thus, if you set the Value property for an option button to True, then the Value properties for all the other option buttons in the group are automatically set to False. All the option buttons in a form or a frame belong to a single grouping.

The Value property has different meaning for the scroll bar controls. At any given time, this property will contain a value that is between whatever the minimum and maximum values are for the scroll bar. This value range is designated by the Min and Max properties.

Enabled

Many controls can be either enabled or disabled at run time by using the Enabled property. If this property is set to True (the default), the control is available to be operated when the program is running. If the Enabled property is set to False, then the control will not be available visible though inoperable. Typically this means that when your program is running, the control is grayed so it cannot be accessed.

Visible

Another property that is common to many different controls is Visible. This property can be set to True or False. It specifies whether the control is actually displayed when your program is running. If a control is invisible (the

Visible property is set to False), the program user cannot access it. Your program code, however, can access it. Using invisible controls comes in handy when you have toggle settings you want to maintain internally (you could use invisible option buttons) or you have a small internal database of information (you could use an invisible list box).

The Tab Order

The tab order has to do with the order in which different controls are selected when your program is running and the Tab key is pressed. Normally, Visual Basic sets the tab order equal to the sequence in which you added controls to your form. Few of us do development sequentially, however, so this tab order may not be acceptable.

To change the tab order, use the TabIndex property. You can set it to any value between 0 (the first control selected) and one less than the number of controls on your form. Thus, if you have six controls on a form, the TabIndex can be any value between 0 and 5. When you explicitly set the TabIndex property, the values of TabIndex for the remaining controls are automatically renumbered.

> **Note**
>
> Some controls, such as a label control, can be given a tab order, but that does not mean the user will be able to select the control by using the Tab key. This is because for most purposes, it makes no sense for the user to select these types of controls.

If there is a control on your form that you don't want (or need) the user to be able to select with the Tab key, you can set the TabStop property for that control to False. Neither the TabStop or TabIndex properties will have any effect if the user selects a control with the mouse.

From Here...

In this chapter, you jumped head-long into the Toolbox, learning how controls are used as an integral part of your programs. You were introduced to the most commonly used controls, as well as to properties they use. In particular, you learned the following:

- How to change control properties when designing and when running your programs.

Tip
To make a control temporarily unavailable, it is best to set the Enabled property to False rather than set the Visible property to False. Doing so leaves the control in place, which makes it easier to remember where your buttons are. Make a control invisible only when you have no intention of the user directly accessing it.

■ How to move, resize, copy, and delete controls.

■ How to use common controls such as command buttons, labels, text boxes, check boxes, option buttons, scroll bars, list boxes, and combo boxes.

■ How to use a frame control to group other controls.

■ How to change common control properties such as `Caption`, `Text`, `Alignment`, `Value`, `Enabled`, and `Visible`.

■ How to change font information, which determines how information is displayed in the controls.

■ How to modify the tab order for controls in a form.

Chapter 4

Variables and Operators

Most computer programs make some sort of calculation in order to operate. These calculations are made using *variables,* which are the building blocks of the calculating portion of your program. Just like different parts of a building may require different sizes of bricks, different portions of your programs require different types of variables.

In this chapter, you will learn about the different types of variables and operators you can use in Visual Basic. One of the marks of a good programmer is the ability to match the right data type with the proper operator to produce the precise result desired. This chapter will teach you the fundamentals you need to increase your skills in this area.

Understanding Data Types

Variables are nothing but storage spaces for values. If you prefer concrete analogies, you can think of them as containers that hold information. They are called variables because their contents can vary—that is, they can be changed.

Variables come in different types (often called *data types*) so you can properly handle different types of information. Because Visual Basic provides different types of variables you can use in your programs, you must learn about them. Only then will you be aware of the many benefits they provide, such as:

- Better memory use in your program
- Faster run time for your program

■ Greater accuracy in calculations

■ Greater readability in program code

Experience has shown that the information used in a program usually falls into one of several well-defined groups. These groups are shown in Table 4.1.

Table 4.1 Visual Basic data types			
Type	**Bytes**	**Suffix**	**Example**
Integer	2	%	LocalCounter% = 5
Long	4	&	BigCounter& = 83727
Single	4	!	ApproxPi! = 3.14
Double	8	#	AccuratePi# = 3.141592654
Currency	8	@	MyDebt = 125948.01
String	*	$	GirlsName$ = "Madaline"
Variant	**	None	Any of the above

*Dependent on the string length.
**Dependent on the type of data stored.

The second column of Table 4.1 shows the amount of computer memory consumed by each variable type. Notice that by using a double-precision variable where an integer would do, you consume four times the necessary memory. Because mathematical operations on variables that consume more memory take longer, your program will run slower when you use a variable type that is larger than necessary.

You may be wondering how to specify the variable type. The most thorough way, from the standpoint of good programming practice, is to explicitly declare the variable, as demonstrated later in this chapter. If, however, you choose not to explicitly declare your variables, you can still specify their type. Add the suffix character shown in column three of Table 4.1 to the variable name and Visual Basic will know that you want that variable to be a specific type. Example variable names are shown in column four.

Standard Variable Types

Most of the data you work with will fit well into one of the standard data types you are about to see. If it doesn't, don't worry; there may be a way to handle it, as you will see in the next section.

Remember that different data types are intended for different types of numbers. Thus, one data type may be designed for values within a particular range, while a different data type will handle an entirely different range. Table 4.2 illustrates the ranges of values that can be supported by the various standard data types.

Table 4.2 Range of Visual Basic data types		
Type	**Largest Negative**	**Largest Positive**
Integer	−32,768	32,767
Long	−2,147,483,648	2,147,483,647
Single	−3.402823^{38}	3.402823^{38}
Double	−1.79769313486232^{308}	1.79769313486232^{308}
Currency	−922,337,203,685,477.5808	922,337,203,685,477.5807
String	0 characters	Approx. 65,000 characters

Integer

Integers are frequently used for counters in loops and for counting any relatively small collection. Integers are whole numbers, sometimes referred to as *counting numbers*. Examples of integers are 1, 2, 3, and so on. An integer cannot be used to represent a number that includes a value to the right of the decimal point, such as .5 or 22.85. Visual Basic has different data types for these types of numbers.

Integers can also be negative numbers such as −4 or −858; such numbers are whole and don't contain a decimal portion.

Long. The Long data type is used anywhere you would normally use an integer, but where the Integer data type would not be sufficient to hold a large enough value. If you had to count to a million, an integer wouldn't do, but a Long data type would be more than sufficient.

Single. The Single data type, also referred to as *single precision,* uses the same amount of memory as the Long data type, but it utilizes that memory in a different way. A single-precision variable can represent a value a little larger than 340,282,300,000,000,000,000,000,000,000,000,000,000.

Because writing down all these zeros can be so time-consuming, a form of shorthand notation was developed for Visual Basic. In this shorthand, that large number is written as 3.402823E38 (notice the *E* in the middle of the number). This shorthand is called *scientific notation.* To convert a number in scientific notation to the more familiar form, simply move the decimal point to the right by the number of places shown after the *E* (in this case, 38). To convert a number to scientific notation, move the decimal point to the position immediately after the first digit and count the number of digits you moved it. Add an *E* to your number and then append the count of how many places the decimal point was moved.

Because Visual Basic understands scientific notation, you can input values in scientific notation. Sometimes, when a number is large enough to warrant it, Visual Basic displays numbers in scientific notation.

A Single data type can represent a very large number, but it cannot represent a large number with precision down to the decimal point. In fact, if you write out the maximum value that a single-precision number can represent, 340,282,300,000,000,000,000,000,000,000,000,000,000, the smallest value you can subtract from this number that has any effect is about 1E32, or 100 quadrillion quadrillion. If you need greater precision, consider using a Double data type.

Double. The Double data type works the same way as the Single data type, but it consumes twice as much memory. It uses the additional memory to provide both greater precision and greater range. Like the Single data type, it exhibits a potential problem in representing extremely large numbers with precision.

The lack of precision is usually not a problem for both the Double and the Single data type. When you frequently deal with very large numbers, you aren't worried about the digits closer to the decimal point. If you had $6,000,000,000,001, would you care much about that $1 at the end? Probably not. The Single and Double data types take advantage of this fact by using their allocated memory to store a number so it can represent very large values—but at the cost of precision.

When Double data types are represented using scientific notation, a *D* is used instead of an *E* as in 1.307674368D12. The *D* lets you know you are working with a Double data type. Other than using a different letter, they work the same as Single data types represented in scientific notation.

Currency. Programs that deal with dollars and cents sometimes need to represent large numbers with high precision. An accounting program may need to keep track of millions or even billions of dollars, yet at the same time it can't afford to lose even a single penny. When making calculations that require both high precision and large values, use the Currency data type.

In many other languages and in older versions of BASIC, programmers used a technique known as *scaling* to represent large dollar and cent values. In scaling you store the value, say 544.35, as pennies by multiplying by 100, so it becomes 54435. When you must reference the value, you divide it by 100, thus returning it to its original form. This technique allows you to use an Integer data type to store a decimal number. Although there are several potential pitfalls in using this technique, until the advent of the Currency data type it was the best option. Visual Basic's Currency data type provides for numbers over 40 million times as large as even a scaled Long data type.

Strings. Some of the data that you use in your programs isn't numeric at all. In fact, most of the information you communicate has nothing to do with numbers. This information, like the text of this book, is in the form of sentences. The sentences are made up of words which are, in turn, composed of characters.

Visual Basic can handle long strings of characters through the String data type. In fact, strings can contain over 64,000 characters. To assign a group of characters to a string variable, just surround the characters with quotation marks. Thus, the following program line assigns the characters "Yellow Dog" to the variable Scourge$:

```
Scourge$ = "Yellow Dog"
```

You can tell a string variable from a numeric one by the dollar sign suffix that is appended to the variable name. Thus, A$, Address$, and PayType$ are all strings. Programmers generally look at a variable such as Address$ and pronounce it as "address string." Because strings are handled differently than numeric data, this pronunciation helps to keep things straight.

No other mainstream computer language allows you to handle strings as easily, or with as much versatility, as Visual Basic does.

Special Data Types

Standard data types don't always meet the special programming needs that come up from time to time. To handle special situations, Visual Basic provides the Variant data type, an innovative approach to data definition. Other special data types are also available, such as data types to handle dates and times.

Variant. The Variant data type gets its name from its ability to vary its format, taking on the form of the data it contains. If you store a string to a Variant, the Variant appears as a String data type and can be manipulated by the string operators. If you store a number to a Variant, it acts like a numeric variable and you can use the arithmetic operators in its manipulation.

While Variants are convenient (in the sense that you don't have to think much to use them), you should avoid them, unless you have a specific need which can't be solved in any reasonable way without their use. It's always better to have a thorough understanding of what your program is doing and why it is doing it. Using Variants is like painting without first scraping, sanding, and priming. If everything under the new paint is okay, you can get away without any extra work. If it's not, then the new paint will soon be a mess and you will be doing the job over.

Date/Time. Strictly speaking, there is no Date/Time data type in Visual Basic. Provisions have been made, however, within the Variant data type for storing a *serial number* representing the date and time.

One serial number is used to store both the date and the time. The valid range of dates is 1-1-0000 to 12-31-9999. In the next chapter, you will see some ways of manipulating the date and time values that can be stored in Variants.

Caution

Because dates prior to 1752 do not take into account the switch from the Julian to the Gregorian calendar, some date calculations that cover long time spans may not calculate properly.

Empty. Empty is really a value, not a type; it is the value of a Variant that has not been initialized. To determine if a Variant has been initialized, use the IsEmpty function within your source code.

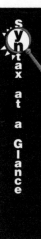

The *IsEmpty* Function

The format of IsEmpty is

    IsEmpty(variant)

Where variant is a variable of the Variant type.

Example

```
If IsEmpty(MyVariantVariable) Then
    MsgBox "This Variant Has Never Been Used"
Else
    MsgBox "This Variant Has Been Used"
End If
```

IsEmpty returns True if the Variant has not been initialized (never used) and False if it has.

There are additional functions for testing Variants to determine the type of value they contain. For in-depth information on their use, see Que's *Using Visual Basic 3*.

Variable Declarations

Has anyone ever given you instructions to do something and after you do it they are upset because what you did wasn't what they wanted you to do? You followed their instructions exactly, and you tell them so. Their response is "But, that's not what I meant!"

The single greatest problem which will plague you as a programmer is getting the computer to do what you mean for it to do (instead of what you tell it to do). Computers are extremely good at following instructions. They do exactly what you tell them to do. Your instructions, therefore, must be both precise and correct.

Visual Basic offers several tools which assist in assuring that what you are telling the computer is what you mean to tell it. One of these tools is *variable declaration*.

Variable declaration is a way of telling Visual Basic about your intended use for a particular variable. If you intend to store someone's name to the variable FirstName$ and declare that fact with Visual Basic before using the variable, Visual Basic will check that the item you are attempting to assign is actually a string of characters and not a number.

Explicit declaration also eliminates another common error—misspellings. Listing 4.1 provides a typical example.

Listing 4.1 Misspelling error.

```
FirstName$ = "Jeffrey"
If FestName$ = "Jeffrey" Then
    MsgBox "It's Jeff!"
EndUnderstanding Data Types    78 If
```

Because you misspelled FirstName, on the second line, your code will never recognize that "Jeffrey" has been assigned. If you use Option Explicit to ensure explicit declarations, you will receive an error when you attempt to run the program. The error message will tell you that the variable FestName is undefined and will even take you to the line on which it appears so you can correct it.

Most novice programmers initially view explicit variable declaration as a nuisance; they feel it takes too much time to declare variables before using them. Using explicit declaration is very important. You will waste far more time trying to track down obscure bugs in your programs due to type errors than you will spend explicitly declaring your variables.

Hopefully you are sold on explicit declaration. To use it, include the line

```
Option Explicit
```

in the Declarations section of each form and module in your project. This tells Visual Basic you will be declaring all variables in advance. If you attempt to use a variable that hasn't been declared, Visual Basic will inform you the next time you try to run your program.

Tip

You can make sure that all your forms and modules include the Option Explicit statement by selecting the **E**nvironment menu item from the **O**ptions menu and setting Require Variable Declaration to Yes.

Dim. You use the Dim statement to declare, or dimension, a variable.

The *Dim* Statement

Dim has several formats. The simplest is:

```
Dim variable1 As type1 [, variable2 As type2]
➥[...variableX As typeY]
```

Dim declares a variable name as a certain type and allocates memory for it.

Example

```
Dim MyVariable as Integer, YourVariable as Currency
```

Caution

Unlike some other programming languages, when explicitly declaring variables in Visual Basic, you must specify the type of each variable beside the variable name, or else render it a Variant by default. Look at the following line:

```
Dim FirstVar, SecondVar as Integer
```

SecondVar will indeed be declared as an integer; FirstVar, however, will not. The following line demonstrates the proper syntax for declaring both variables as integers:

```
Dim FirstVar as Integer, SecondVar as Integer
```

Static. When a procedure is called in which a variable has been declared, the variable is initialized. Each time the procedure is called, the variable is again initialized. If you want to retain the value of the variable, declare it as Static.

A variable declared Static retains its value between procedure calls. For example, you declare a Static variable MyStatic@ in a function. You call that procedure for the first time, store the value 55.75 to the variable, and then exit the procedure. The next time you call the procedure and refer to the variable MyStatic@, it still contains the value 55.75.

Global. If you declare a variable within a module, that variable is only visible to the procedures within that module. Procedures in other modules cannot access it. The accessibility of a variable's value is referred to as the variable's *scope.*

By declaring a variable Global, you are telling Visual Basic its scope is global, or available to all modules and forms.

The *Static* Statement

Static has several formats. The simplest is:

```
Static variable as type
```

Static is used at the procedure level in order to retain the value of the variable between procedure calls.

Example

```
Static MyVariable as String
```

The *Global* Statement

Global has several formats. The simplest is:

```
Global variable1 As type1 [,variable2 As type2]
➡[...,variableX As typeY]
```

Global is used in the Declarations section of the startup module, or of an independent global module, to make variables available to all procedures in all forms and modules.

Example

```
Global EveryonesVariable as Long
```

Visual Basic limits the scope of a variable to the form or module in which it is declared. There are several reasons why all variables aren't available everywhere in the program.

By limiting the scope of a variable, you minimize the amount of memory required at any one moment during the execution of your program. While a form's procedure code is executing, all its variables are held in memory. Upon completion, Visual Basic recovers the memory space used by these variables. This space can be significant, especially in large programs.

Limited scope helps prevent the introduction of bugs into your programs too. If you use a variable in a procedure associated with one form, you can use a variable by the same name in another procedure, associated with another form, and the two won't be confused. Their values will be stored in different places in memory.

If all variables were global and you accidentally used the same variable name in two places, your program may produce undesired results. For example, you may be using the variable for a particular purpose somewhere in your code, and then you execute a different procedure that uses the same variable. The variable would still contain the value it had in the first case, which may not be anticipated by the second piece of code, thus leading to an error.

Understanding Operators

Variables are the raw material of your programs. You will work with that raw material using operators. Fortunately, Visual Basic has one of the richest sets of operators available. This operator set makes the job of programming, using Visual Basic, much simpler.

As you learned at the beginning of this chapter, variables are so named because their value can change—that is, they can vary. This flexibility is the feature that makes them so useful. There are many ways to change the value contained in a variable.

When working with variables, the kind of manipulation you perform is defined by the *operator*. The operator is the symbol that defines what type of operation should take place in the equation. If there is only one variable being operated on, it is called the *operand*. If there is more than one variable, they are referred to collectively as the *operands*.

Arithmetic Operators

The most common category of operations are those involving arithmetic. You probably know most of the arithmetic operations, but Visual Basic includes some useful ones with which you may not be familiar. Table 4.3 lists the arithmetic operators you can use in Visual Basic.

Table 4.3 Arithmetic operators	
Operator	**Operation**
+	Addition
–	Subtraction
·	Multiplication

(continues)

Table 4.3 Continued	
Operator	**Operation**
/	Division
^	Exponentation
\	Integer division
Mod	Modulus

Examples of addition, subtraction, multiplication, and division are given in Table 4.4.

Table 4.4 Basic math examples	
Equation	**Result**
4 + 5	9
7 - 9	-2
4.4 * 2	8.8
10 / 4	2.5

The Exponentation Operator. Sometimes you may need to multiply a number by itself, such as 2 * 2. Sometimes you may need to multiply a number by itself more than once, such as 2 * 2 * 2 * 2. In many scientific, engineering, and financial applications, you may even be required to multiply a number by itself hundreds of times. In these cases, writing out the multiplication isn't very convenient. This is where exponentiation comes into play.

Exponentiation is a shorthand method of multiplying a number repeatedly. 2 * 2 is written as 2 ^ 2 and pronounced as "two raised to the second power". 3 * 3 * 3 * 3 becomes 3 ^ 4 or "three raised to the fourth power". And 6 ^ 184, or "six raised to the one hundred eighty fourth power," you don't want to write out.

You also can raise a number to a fractional exponent, as in 3 ^ 1.5. Visual Basic can also do this, as well as handle numbers raised to negative exponents. In the next chapter, you'll see functions that, when combined with the fundamental operators of this chapter, make Visual Basic an excellent choice for the solution of scientific and financial problems.

Table 4.5 illustrates how exponentiation is used in Visual Basic.

Table 4.5 Exponentiation examples	
Equation	**Result**
2 ^ 10	1024
-3 ^ 4	81
4.4 ^ 2.2	1,649.16224
2 ^ -2	.5

Integer Operators. Integer division, represented by a backslash, takes two values as operands and returns an integer as the result. If you use a noninteger as one or both of the operands, the noninteger will be converted to an integer first and then the division will be performed. The result is always an integer.

Be careful not to confuse integer division with normal division, which is represented by a forward slash. Each type of division produces different results. Table 4.6 provides several examples of how integer division is done.

Table 4.6 Integer division examples		
Equation	**Rounded Equivalent**	**Result**
8 \ 2	8 \ 2	4
9 \ 2.6	9 \ 3	3
-9 \ 2.6	-9 \ 3	-3
4.4 \ 2	4 \ 2	2

Remember when you were first learning how to divide? The answers you got to a problem such as "six divided by five" were "one remainder one". The remainder is what is left over after the division. The Mod operator returns the remainder of a division operation.

Combining the Mod operator with integer division can yield an answer in the same form as if you did the division manually and phrased your answer with a remainder.

Like integer division, the operands are rounded to integers prior to the Mod operation being performed. Also, as with integer division, the result is always an integer. Table 4.7 lists examples of using the Mod operator.

Table 4.7 Modulus examples		
Equation	**Rounded Equivalent**	**Result**
5 Mod 5	5 Mod 5	0
5 Mod 4	5 Mod 4	1
5.5 Mod 1.5	6 Mod 2	0
5.5 Mod 5	6 Mod 5	1

Comparison Operators

The comparison operators are used when you want to know the magnitude of one variable compared to another. "Does variable1 contain a value which is larger, smaller, or exactly equal to variable2?" is the kind of question to which a comparison operator will provide an answer.

The result of any comparison can only be True or False. Table 4.8 lists the different comparison operators.

Table 4.8 Comparison operators	
Operator	**Operation**
=	Equal
<	Less than
>	Greater than
<=	Less than or equal
>=	Greater than or equal
<>	Not equal

Tip
String comparisons, by default, are case-sensitive. The strings "joe" and "Joe" are not equal. To make string comparisons case-insensitive (where "joe" would equal "Joe"), place the line

Option Compare Text

in the Declarations section of the form or module containing the comparison. (For more information see the Visual Basic on-line help.)

These operators can be used on strings as well as numbers.

The Equal operator is fairly straightforward. Just remember that *equal* means exactly equal. If two values differ by even the slightest amount, they will not be evaluated as equal. The two values 4.0 and 4.0000000001 may look the same when shown on your form (due to formatting), but the values in memory are different and therefore not equal.

When using the Greater Than and Less Than operators, remember that any negative number is less than any positive number. As an illustration, –1,000,000 is less than 100, and less than 5, and even less than .0000001. Remember, too, that –50 is less than –5.

This is easy to remember if you picture all numbers placed on a number line, like you used to use in elementary school. The line has 0 in the middle, the positive numbers (1,2,3, and so on) to the right, and the negative numbers (–1,–2,–3, and so on) heading off to the left. Pick any two numbers on this number line. The one on the left is always less, and the one to the right is always more.

The Not Equal operator will tell you if any two variables are different, even by the slightest amount. Not equal can be used to determine if two dates or times are the same, if two files have identical names, or if the length of two files differ. It can be used anywhere you need to know if there is the slightest difference.

Less Than or Equal combines two questions into one: "Is value1 less than value2", OR "Is value1 equal to value2"? OR is shown in capitals to emphasize that if either of the conditions is met, the statement is True. Greater Than or Equal works in a similar (but opposite) manner.

Each comparison has a converse, or opposite. For the Equal operator it is Not Equal. By testing for one of the conditions, you know the result of the other. If a number is equal to another, it can't be not equal at the same time. The same is true of the converse pairs shown in Table 4.9.

Table 4.9 Converse comparison pairs

Operator	Converse
=	<>
<	>=
>	<=

Knowing about converse pairs allows you more flexibility in structuring the logical flow of your programs. Instead of writing

```
If Not(BigVariable <= SmallVariable) Then
```

you can write

```
If BigVariable > SmallVariable Then
```

which is much more readable. The two produce exactly the same result in all situations.

Logical Operators

You use logical operators to build more complex logical constructs. For example, if you have a group of individuals and you want to locate all single red-headed males who are between the ages of 20 and 30 and who don't have a pet, logical operators provide the means. The following demonstrates:

```
(MaritalStatus = "S") And (HairColor = "Red") And (Age >= 20) And
(Age <= 30) And (Pet = "None")
```

Logical operators allow you to apply Boolean logic to your data, determining a final solution that is either True or False. Visual Basic provides four logical operators, as shown in Table 4.10.

Table 4.10 Logical operators	
Operator	**Operation**
Not	Not (or the logical opposite of)
And	And
Eqv	Equivalent
Imp	Implication
Or	Or
Xor	Exclusive Or

There are two ways to understand the results of a logical operation. The first involves looking at the operation graphically, and the other involves truth tables. Both approaches are instructive, and in several of the following sections both approaches are used.

In a truth table all possible combinations of values are listed, and the result of the logical operation is listed next to each combination.

The *AND* Operator. AND returns a True value only if both operands are True; otherwise the result is False. Table 4.11 and figure 4.1 provide explanations of how the AND operator functions.

Table 4.11 Truth table for *AND*		
A	**B**	**A AND B**
True	True	True
True	False	False
False	True	False
False	False	False

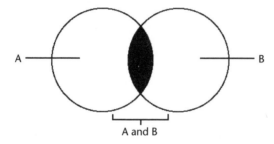

Fig. 4.1
Pictorial representation of AND.

Listing 4.2 shows a typical use of the AND operator.

Listing 4.2 Use of *AND*.

```
If (FirstName = "Tony") And (LastName = "Carpenter") Then
    MsgBox "Found Tony"
Else
    MsgBox "Tony could not be found!"

End If
```

Notice the use of parentheses in the listing. Operations within parentheses are performed first, and then the results are used in further calculations. This technique ensures that operations are performed in the order you intend. In the preceding example, FirstName is compared with "Tony", and LastName is compared with "Carpenter" ; then the results are compared.

The *EQV* Operator. EQV returns a True value only if both operands are equal; otherwise the result is False. Table 4.12 provides an explanation of how the EQV operator functions.

Table 4.12 Truth table for *EQV*		
A	**B**	**A *EQV* B**
True	True	True
True	False	False
False	True	False
False	False	True

Listing 4.3 shows a typical use of the EQV operator.

Listing 4.3 Use of *EQV*.

```
If total Eqv overflow Then
     DoError          'Signify error condition
End If
```

In all numeric situations, the EQV operator is the same as using an equal sign in a comparison. EQV does not act as a comparison operator for strings, however.

The *OR* Operator. OR returns a True value if either of the operands are True. It only returns a False result if both of the operands are False. Table 4.13 and figure 4.2 provide explanations of how the OR operator functions.

Table 4.13 Truth table for *OR*		
A	**B**	**A *OR* B**
True	True	True
True	False	True
False	True	True
False	False	False

Fig. 4.2
Pictorial representation of OR.

A OR B

Listing 4.4 provides an example of how you could use the OR operator in a program.

Listing 4.4 Use of *OR*.

```
If FirstName = "Beth" OR FirstName = "Ginger" Then
    MsgBox "Female"
End If
```

The *XOR* Operator. The XOR operator returns a True value when only one of the operands is True. The XOR operator returns a False value whenever both operands are the same—whether they are both True or both False. Table 4.14 and figure 4.3 provide explanations of how the XOR operator functions.

Table 4.14 Truth table for *XOR*		
A	**B**	**A *XOR* B**
True	True	False
True	False	True
False	True	True
False	False	False

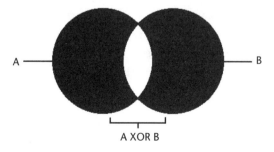

Fig. 4.3
Pictorial representation of XOR.

A XOR B

Listing 4.5 provides an example of how you could use the XOR operator in a program.

Listing 4.5 Use of *XOR*.

```
If (FirstName = "Tony") XOR (LastName = "Carpenter") Then
    MsgBox "Same first name or same last name but not both."
Else
    MsgBox "None with just the same first or last name."
End If
```

The *IMP* Operator. IMP is the local implication operator. It returns a False value only if the second operand is False and the first is True; otherwise the result is True. Table 4.15 provides an explanation of how the IMP operator functions.

Table 4.15 Truth table for *IMP*		
A	**B**	**A EQV B**
True	True	True
True	False	False
False	True	True
False	False	True

Listing 4.6 shows a typical use of the IMP operator.

Listing 4.6 Use of *IMP*.

```
If Price > 100000 Imp Pay > 60000 Then
    MsgBox "Applicant doesn't qualify"        'Pay not high enough
Else
    MsgBox "Applicant appears to qualify"
End If
```

The *NOT* Operator. Unlike the other logical operators, the NOT operator does not require two operands. Instead, it performs a logical negation of a value. In other words, a True value is changed to False, and vice versa. Listing 4.7 gives an example of how you could use the NOT operator in an equation.

Listing 4.7 Use of *NOT*.

```
While Not EOF(2)
    GetInfo
    DisplayInfo
    GetChanges
    UpdateInfo
Wend
Wend
```

String Operators

Earlier in this chapter, you learned about comparison operators and how they can be used to compare numeric values. Comparison operators also can be used with strings, and then the result used in further computations.

In addition, Visual Basic provides a way to *concatenate,* or combine, strings together. Consider the following code fragment:

```
FirstName$ = John
LastName$ = Davis
FullName$ = FirstName$ &    & LastName$
rtName$ = LastName$ & ,   & FirstName$
```

When this code is executed, the `FullName$` variable will contain the characters `"John Davis"`, and the `SortName$` variable will contain `"Davis, John"`.

You will find that strings, and string operations, are involved in virtually every program you can imagine.

From Here...

The forms and controls of previous chapters are the foundation on which you will construct your Visual Basic programs. This chapter presented the raw materials (variables and data types) and some fundamental tools (operators) that you will use in putting your program code together in later chapters. In particular you learned the following:

- What data types are available.

- What data types are appropriate for different types of data.

- How to declare variables.

- What operators are available.

- How comparison and logical operators work.

- How to work with strings.

Chapter 5

Using Built-In Functions

Visual Basic offers a rich set of built-in functions for manipulating dates, times, strings, and numbers. Built-in functions are important because they save you time and effort—you don't need to reinvent the wheel.

In this chapter, you will learn how to use functions in your programs. You will learn the syntax and nuances of various functions that will make your programming life easier. By the time you reach the end of this chapter, you will know how functions are used.

There are many Visual Basic functions, but not all could be covered in this chapter. All the fundamental functions you need to develop most of your program, however, are included. Some of the functions that are not discussed in this chapter include financial calculations, advanced mathematical operations (such as transcendental functions), functions for navigating through the DOS file structure, functions for manipulating DOS files and attributes, error-handling functions, and functions for use in the manipulation of Visual Basic objects such as control arrays.

The Benefits of Functions

Recognizing the benefits of using built-in functions is easy. For example, imagine how long it would take to accomplish the seemingly simple task of determining whether today is Monday. You would have to figure out how to get the date from your PC, find a formula for calculating the day of the week given that date, and write a small program to implement it. But Visual Basic's Weekday function returns the day of the week in one easy step.

To continue the example, if there weren't built-in functions for working with dates, you would have to buy or borrow reference material on PC internals in order to know where and how the date is stored. You would also need to figure out a way to access the specific memory location containing the date and time information—not an easy task since Visual Basic has no inherent means of accessing a specific memory location. There are third-party tools to give you access to memory, but you would still need a formula to calculate the day of the week. Even if you already had these items, it would take at least an hour to write the program and test it. In contrast, it takes only a moment to find the built-in function you need and incorporate it in your program.

Date and Time Functions

How many days have passed since your birth? On what day of the week will Christmas fall next year? How long until your anniversary? When will your home mortgage be paid off? The answer to these questions requires the ability to work with dates.

To determine how many days have passed since your birth, you must subtract your birth date from the current date. Visual Basic has a function to calculate the difference between two dates; you'll see an example of it later in this chapter. Visual Basic also has functions that allow you to answer the other questions as well.

Visual Basic's date functions work with dates ranging from before 1,800 years ago to more than 8,000 years in the future.

Time is important to everyone on some scale. For a military operation, accuracy is often required to the second—or less; for a busy executive, every minute counts. Most people, however, are probably concerned with at least the hour. Even while you are on vacation you must stay conscious of the date and time, or you may be late returning to your more hectic life.

It's no wonder then that PCs keep track of both the date and time. Your PC has an internal clock that Visual Basic can reference in order to provide a fairly accurate time (see the sidebar).

Syntax at a Glance

Accuracy of Time

The clock inside your PC is not a highly accurate chronograph; it is possible for it to be off by even a few seconds a day. For some applications this may not be acceptable. For the majority of users, however, it is quite acceptable. It all depends on the precision you need.

Simply noting the setting of the sun each evening is adequate for precision of days. A sundial provides precision of hours. A pendulum provides the basis for accurately marking the passing of minutes. A wristwatch is sufficient for seconds. A digital watch often provides stopwatch accuracy down to hundredths of a second. Mankind's quest for precision in the measurement of time has taken us so far we can measure the emissions of the cesium-133 atom to form the basis of a clock that provides accuracy beyond billionths of a second. Time can be measured with different precision.

Where does Visual Basic fit into this continuum of precision? Visual Basic's time-related functions provide precision to the second and can be used to get the current second, minute, hour, day, month, or year.

Visual Basic provides a variety of functions that allow you to access and manipulate both the date and time. Each function typically returns or uses the date and time stored in a variable using the Variant data type (see Chapter 4). This provides you with information you can readily use in your programs.

How Visual Basic Stores Dates and Times

If you started a stopwatch at this moment and stopped it in 315,360,000 seconds, how much older would you be? Because humans don't have the lightening fast calculating speed of computers, it isn't very easy for us to make such calculations. With the aid of a calculator, you'll quickly see that you would be about 10 years older (not accounting for leap years).

What significant historical event occurred approximately 728,500 days ago? Again, most of us are at a loss. A properly programmed computer, however, would quickly determine the year as 0 AD. With that information you know that either the birth or death of Christ was the event (depending on which religious scholars you question).

Visual Basic handles date ranges of this magnitude quite handily by storing dates and times as a serial number in a double-precision number. Everything to the left of the decimal point represents the date, and everything to the right represents the time. You may remember from Chapter 4 that the range of numbers that can be stored in this data type is quite large; VB can handle dates that cover over a 10,000 year range.

Determining Today's Date

The Date function is the starting point for many calculations involving dates. For example, if you want to know how long ago a certain date was or how far in the future a certain date will be, you must start with the current date.

The *Date* Function

The format of Date is

```
Date
```

which returns a Variant data type (Variant Type 7).

Example

```
Dim TodaysDate As Variant
TodaysDate = Date
```

Remember that when you use Date, the date returned is the date stored in the PC's internal clock. If the date stored in the PC is wrong, then Date will obviously not return the correct date.

Determining the Current Time

If you must know the current time of day, use Time.

Note

Your PC contains an internal clock. Like a quartz watch, the internal clock of your PC is based on the vibration of a quartz crystal providing good short-term accuracy. The clock in most PCs is accurate to about plus or minus 15 seconds per month. This means that over time the PC's clock, such as a watch, can drift and require resetting.

To change the time or date stored in your PC's internal clock use the Date/Time icon in the Windows Control Panel.

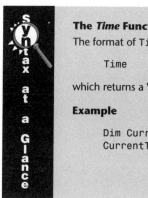

The *Time* Function

The format of Time is

    Time

which returns a Variant data type (Variant Type 7).

Example

    Dim CurrentTime As Variant
    CurrentTime = Time

Because Time returns the value stored in the PC's internal clock, as with Date, if the PC's clock is incorrect, then the value returned by Time will also be incorrect.

Getting Both the Time and Date

Sometimes you need both the current date and the current time. Although you can use both the Date and Time functions, there is a simpler way. You can use the Now function, which combines both Date and Time functions.

The *Now* Function

The format of Now is

    Now

which returns a Variant data type (Variant Type 7).

Example

    Dim TimeAndDate As Variant
    TimeAndDate = Now

Now is also convenient for timing the execution of your program. To find out how long part of your program takes to execute, use the code in Listing 5.1.

Listing 5.1 Timing your program.

```
StartTime = Now

    'code to be timed here

TotalTime = Now - StartTime
```

Make sure that the section you are timing doesn't contain anything that will depend on user input (such as a button press or text entry), because it will distort the timing (unless of course, you want to time how long it takes for the user to respond).

Because the shortest amount of time Visual Basic can measure is one second, and because the CPU in your computer can execute thousands of lines of VB code per second, how can you time how long only a very few lines will take to execute? The answer is that you can't, at least not directly.

The pseudo-stopwatch, Visual Basic's Now function, has the same problem a real stopwatch has when trying to time an event that happens quickly. Its resolution is not fine enough to accurately time the event. For example, if you wanted to time how long it takes a car, traveling at a constant high speed, to go ten feet, you couldn't do it directly. The error incurred by the lack of precision with which you start and stop your stopwatch will introduce too much inaccuracy for a valid result.

By averaging the speed of the car over a longer distance, however, say 5,280 feet (a mile), and then dividing that time by the ratio of the desired distance to the measured distance (10/5280), you get the length of time for the car to travel only ten feet—something you couldn't measure directly.

You can use the same technique with Visual Basic. If you have a sequence of instructions you want to time, place them inside of a For...Next loop. Execute the instructions hundreds or thousands of times, and time how long it takes to complete. Take that time and divide it by the number of times you executed the block of code. This will give you an approximation of the length of time necessary to complete just the few instructions.

> **Note**
>
> Because the For...Next loop consumes some processor time, your calculation will contain some error. The amount of error may not be important. For example, when you compare two alternative ways of doing the same thing, both methods will suffer from the same inaccuracy and therefore can be compared.
>
> In addition, there are many different factors which affect the execution speed of a piece of code. Factors as diverse as the type of CPU, the frequency at which the processor is clocked, the access speed of the memory in the computer, whether the computer has cache memory, and even the speed of the hard disk drive can influence how long it takes your program to run.

The moral of the story is: Don't use your timings as hard fact unless they are accompanied by information on all the factors which influence them. This type of timing is most useful when used for comparative purposes on a single PC.

Extracting Part of the Date

Sometimes you only need part of the date. For questions such as "Is today Wednesday?" and "Is this 1995?" Visual Basic provides the following four functions for extracting only the part of the date in which you're interested:

- Year returns the year portion of the date. (The range can be 100 to 9999.)

- Month returns an integer from 1 to 12 (January to December).

- Day returns the day of the month (1 to 31).

- Weekday returns the day of the week represented by a number from 1 to 7 (Sunday to Saturday).

If someone asks you "When was the last time you used your PC?" would you answer "Last 3."? No, of course not. For calculation purposes, the integers returned by the Weekday function work just fine; for display, however, they just won't do.

The code in Listing 5.2 can be used to provide an English translation of the number returned from the Weekday function.

Listing 5.2 *Weekday* function.

```
DOWNum = Weekday(Now)
DOWString$ = Choose(DOWNum, "Sunday", "Monday", "Tuesday",
Â"Wednesday", "Thursday", "Friday", "Saturday")
```

In this example, the Choose function selects one of the following variables based on DOWNum. If DOWNum = 1 then Choose selects the first one listed— "Sunday". If DOWNum = 2 then Choose selects "Monday".

Extracting Part of the Time

If you were only interested in a portion of the time (for example, the hour), you could use Visual Basic's string functions to separate out the part in which you were interested.

The *Year, Month, Day,* and *Weekday* Functions

The format used by these functions is

```
Type(DateVariant)
```

This function returns an integer. *Type* is any of the following: Year, Month, Day, or Weekday. *DateVariant* is a Variant which contains a valid date or a function which returns a Variant containing a valid date.

Examples

```
Dim ThisYear As Integer
ThisYear = Year(Date)
```

After this is executed, ThisYear will contain an integer value of the current year, such as 1994.

```
Dim ThisMonth As Integer
ThisMonth = Month(Now)
```

After this is executed, ThisMonth will contain an integer value of the current month, such as 12.

```
Dim ThisDay As Integer
ThisDay = Day(Date)
```

After this is executed, ThisDay will contain an integer value of the current day, such as 30.

```
Dim DayOfWeek As Integer
DayOfWeek = Weekday(Now)
```

In this example, the returned integer value will be in the range 1 to 7, where 1 represents Sunday, 2 represents Monday, and so on through 7, which represents Saturday.

Given the time 7:45:05 you could use InStr to find the first and second colon. Then, depending on which portion of the time you were interested in, you could use the Mid function to obtain that part.

An easier way, however, is by using any of the following functions: Hour, Minute, and Second.

Differences Between Two Dates

Earlier in this chapter, you learned that you can use one of Visual Basic's built-in functions to determine the number of days since you were born. DateDiff is that function. DateDiff returns the number of days between two dates. If the first date is actually after the second, then DateDiff will return a negative number.

The *Hour, Minute,* and *Second* Functions

The format is

    Type(DateVariant)

Where *Type* is any of the following: Hour, Minute, or Second. *DateVariant* is a variable of the Variant type which contains either a valid time or a function that returns a Variant containing a valid time.

Examples

```
Dim ThisHour As Integer
ThisHour = Hour(Now)
```

When this example is executed, ThisHour will contain an integer value of the current hour. The value will be between 0 and 23.

```
Dim ThisMinute As Integer
ThisMinute = Minute(Now)
```

When this example is executed, ThisMinute will contain an integer value of the current minute. The value will be between 0 and 59.

```
Dim ThisSecond As Integer
ThisSecond = Second(Now)
```

When this example is executed, ThisSecond will contain an integer value of the current second. The value will be between 0 and 59.

The *DateDiff* Function

The format is

    DateDiff(interval, startdate, enddate)

Where *interval* is a string representing the units in which you want to measure the difference. They are:

Year	yyyy
Quarter	q
Month	m
Week	ww
DayofYear	y
Weekday	w
Day	d
Hour	h
Minute	n
Second	s

Example

```
Dim NumDays As Variant
NumDays = DateDiff("d", Now, "6/5/86")
```

This example calculates the number of days since June 5, 1986.

To show how the `DateDiff` function can work for you, you will create a date calculator. Figure 5.1 shows the bare-bones form layout for the calculator. Notice that you will need to use the following controls in the form:

- One command button

- Four labels

- Two text boxes

- One dropdown combo box (Dropdown list style)

Next, set the form and control properties shown in Table 5.1.

Fig. 5.1
The bare-bones form layout for the date calculator.

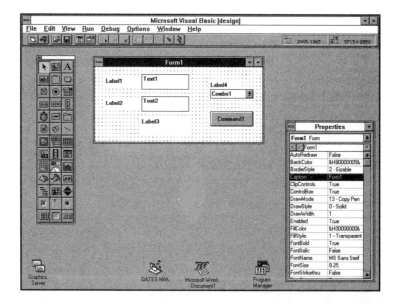

Table 5.1 Date calculator properties

Object	Property	Value
Form	Caption	Date Calculator
Command1	Caption	Calculate Now
Label1	Caption Alignment	Begin Date Right Justify
Label2	Caption Alignment	End Date Right Justify

Object	Property	Value
Label3	Caption	(Delete caption)
Label4	Caption	Interval
Text1	Text	(Delete text)
Text2	Text	(Delete text)
Combo1	Style	Dropdown list

Next, add the double-click on the command button control and make sure the Code window contains the code shown in Listing 5.3. Then you can close the Code window.

Listing 5.3 Code for the date calculator command button.

```
Sub Command1_Click ()
  If Not IsDate(Text1) Or Not IsDate(Text2) Then
    MsgBox "Please make sure the Begin and End dates are valid",
    ➥48, "Date Calculator"
    Exit Sub
  End If
  Select Case Combo1
    Case "Years"
      DiffType = "yyyy"
      DiffUnits = " Year difference"
    Case "Months"
      DiffType = "m"
      DiffUnits = " Month difference"
    Case Else
      DiffType = "d"
      DiffUnits = " Day difference"
  End Select
  Label3 = DateDiff(Difftype, Text1, Text2) & DiffUnits
End Sub
```

Now double-click on the form itself, and make sure the Code window contains the code shown in Listing 5.4.

Listing 5.4 Code for the date calculator form.

```
Sub Form_Load ()
  Combo1.AddItem "Years"
  Combo1.AddItem "Months"
  Combo1.AddItem "Days"
End Sub
```

When you are finished, the form should look like figure 5.2.

Fig. 5.2

The finished form
layout for the date
calculator.

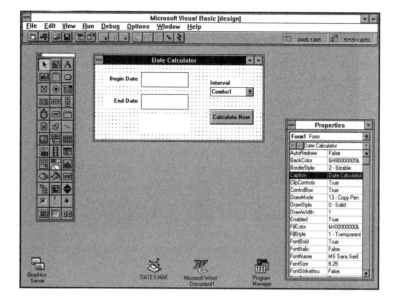

This project uses a few functions you won't learn about until later in the chapter, so here's a quick explanation of their purpose.

- IsDate determines whether a variable contains a valid date. It is used here to make sure that DateDiff isn't called with an invalid date.

- MsgBox displays a message in a dialog box. The first string in the argument is the text of the message, the last string is the title of the message box, the number between the two determines which buttons and which icons, if any, are displayed. The value 48 produces an OK button and exclamation point icon. (This function will be covered in Chapter 8.)

When you run the program, you can enter dates in the Begin and End Date fields, and choose a type of interval from the Interval list. Figure 5.3 shows an example of how the program operates.

Deriving a Date

To go the other way when you have a date and want to find a date in the future, use the DateAdd function.

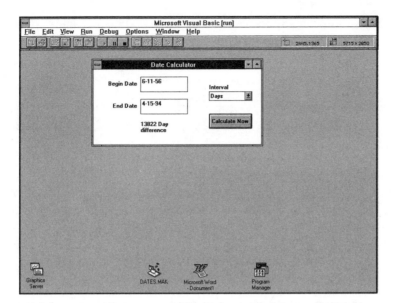

Fig. 5.3
Running the date
calculator.

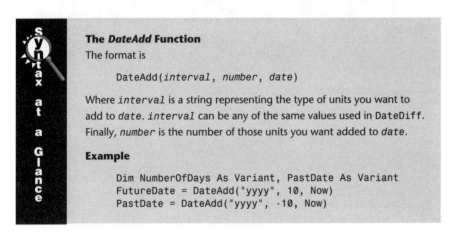

The *DateAdd* Function

The format is

        DateAdd(*interval*, *number*, *date*)

Where *interval* is a string representing the type of units you want to
add to *date*. *interval* can be any of the same values used in DateDiff.
Finally, *number* is the number of those units you want added to *date*.

Example

```
Dim NumberOfDays As Variant, PastDate As Variant
FutureDate = DateAdd("yyyy", 10, Now)
PastDate = DateAdd("yyyy", -10, Now)
```

String Functions

To begin the discussion of string functions, you are going to take a short trip
into the workings of your computer.

Computers store all their information (even strings) as binary numbers.
Binary means one of two states—either *On* or *Off*, *1* or *0*. Computers work
in binary because the electronic switches of which they're made are only
capable of storing a 1 or a 0 at any particular location.

The binary numbering system is also referred to as the *base 2* numbering system. You are accustomed to working in base 10. The value following the word *base* is the number of different values any one digit may have in that numbering system.

In the decimal system (base 10), each digit can have a value from 0 to 9—that's ten possible values. In base two, there are only two possible values—0 or 1.

To count in decimal, you start with a single digit. That digit contains the value 0. As you increment your count, you increase the value in that first digit. When you reach the maximum value for that digit, you reset it to 0 and increment the digit to the left. This process continues as long as necessary. Counting in base 2 follows the same rules, except there are fewer values to use in the digits. The first few binary numbers are shown in Table 5.2.

Binary	Decimal
000	0
001	1
010	2
011	3
100	4
101	5
110	6
111	7

Table 5.2 Counting in binary

You can see how numbers could be stored using this system. But how does this relate to strings?

Characters are stored using a numeric code. By representing a character with a number, that number can be stored and later retrieved by the computer. When displayed, it is converted back into the character so that you can understand it. Table 5.3 shows a part of the list of characters and the values used by the computer to represent them.

Table 5.3 Codes used to represent characters

Character	Decimal	Binary
1	31	0011111
2	30	0100000
3	33	0100001
A	65	1000001
B	66	1000010
C	67	1000011
D	68	1000100
a	97	1100001
b	98	1100010
c	99	1100011
d	100	1100100

In order for computers made by different manufacturers to communicate with one another, a standard code was necessary for the representation of information. The American National Standards Institute (ANSI) has developed a code with values ranging from 0 to 255 which represent numbers, characters, and codes for special purposes such as carriage returns and line feeds. Windows, and hence Visual Basic, support a significant subset of this ANSI code. To see the ANSI codes and their characters, search on-line help for ASCII and select ANSI Character Set.

The first commonly used code for the interchange of computer information was ASCII (American Standard Code for Information Interchange). ASCII has codes only for the values 0 through 127. By the time Windows was developed, the need for additional symbols (not representable in ASCII) had necessitated a new standard. The ANSI standard was adopted to incorporate accented characters. The common characters typed on the keyboard are represented the same in ANSI as in ASCII.

> **Note**
>
> Take another look at the values in Table 5.3. Notice that there are different numeric values for upper- and lowercase letters. When Visual Basic sorts strings, it normally does so by using the numeric code assigned to each letter. Thus, those characters with the lowest ANSI values come first. That's why, when Visual Basic lists items alphabetically (in a sorted list box, for example), text beginning with a number appears before text beginning with a character, and uppercase letters appear before lowercase letters.

Comparing Strings

Visual Basic provides the StrComp function which allows you to quickly determine if two strings are equal. What about the following strings, however:

```
This is a test string.
THIS IS A TEST STRING.
```

If you use the normal comparison operators (see Chapter 4) to do a comparison, these strings are not considered equal. With StrComp, however, you can instruct it to ignore the case of the letters in the string—it all depends on your needs. (If StrComp takes the case of the letters into account, it is considered *case-sensitive*.)

The *StrComp* Function

The format of StrComp is

```
StrComp(string1, string2, [comparison type])
```

Where *string1* and *string2* are the strings to compare and a *comparison type* of 0 performs a case-sensitive compare while a *comparison type* of 1 performs the comparison without regard to case. If the *comparison type* is omitted, then the default type specified for the module (using an Option Compare statement) is used.

The return values are:

```
-1 if string1 < string2
 0 if string1 = string2
 1 if string1 > string2
```

Example

```
Dim StringCompResults As Variant
StringCompResults = StrComp("Test this", "TEST THIS", 1)
```

StringCompResults will contain a 0 because it was instructed to perform a case-insensitive comparison.

Converting Strings

More often than not, you will need to make certain conversions in text strings used in your programs. For example, you may need to ensure that a last name entered in a text box contains an initial uppercase character or that a variable is stored in all uppercase so an exact match can be made. Visual Basic's text conversion functions provide the means for easily manipulating strings.

Converting the Case of a String. For switching entire strings to all upper- or lowercase, the functions LCase and UCase work well. Pass the string to be converted to one of these functions, and a string is returned which is guaranteed to be all upper- or lowercase (depending on which function is used).

To convert just a single character, separate that character, convert it, and then splice it back in. Listing 5.5 shows an example of capitalizing the initial letter of a word using UCase.

Listing 5.5 Conversion of a single character.

```
LowerCaseString = "herberger"
InitialUpper = UCase(Left$(LowerCaseString,1)) &
ÂMid$(LowerCaseString,2)
```

Converting Characters to Values. You can use the Asc function to convert a single character to its ANSI value. Asc is short for ASCII. As you have already learned, Windows uses ANSI characters, though ANSI is based primarily on ASCII. For compatibility reasons, the Asc function was not renamed. Asc returns an integer value which is the ANSI value of first character in a string.

The *Asc* Function
The format of Asc is

  Asc(*string*)

This function returns an integer equal to the ANSI value of the first character of the passed *string*.

Example

```
Dim ANSIValue As Integer
ANSIValue = Asc("C")
```

When this code is executed, ANSIValue will contain the value 67.

Converting Values to Characters. The Chr$ function does just the opposite of Asc. It converts a number into an ANSI character.

When you were a child, did you ever have a secret decoder ring? The secret decoder ring was used to implement a simple substitution cipher. A substitution cipher works by replacing each character in the original message with a substitute. To decode the secret message, just reverse the process by replacing each substitute with the original character.

You can use Chr$ and Asc to encrypt text in this manner. To test this out, follow these steps:

1. Create a new Visual Basic project.

2. Place two text boxes, named Text1 and Text2, on the form.

3. Double-click the form. You will see the Code window appear.

4. Make sure the Click procedure is chosen in the Proc field.

5. Place the information in Listing 5.6 into the Code window.

6. Close the Code window.

You can now run the program. You should type some text into Text1 and then click the form. The encrypted version will appear in Text2.

Listing 5.6 Encryption using _Chr$_ & _Asc._

```
Text2 = ""
For LocalCounter = 1 to Len(Text1)
   Text2 = Text2 & Chr$(Asc(Mid$(Text1,LocalCounter,1))+3)
Next LocalCounter
```

The _Chr$_ Function
The format of Chr$ is

   Chr$(*number*)

This function returns the ANSI equivalent character, as a string, for *number*.

Example

```
Dim CharacterString As String
CharacterString$ = Chr$(67)
```

When this code is executed, CharacterString$ will contain the letter C.

Converting a String to a Number. There will be times when you want to convert a string to a number. This comes in handy when you get input from a user in the form of a string, but you must convert it to a number to process it further. (This was done in the calculator examples in Chapters 1 and 2.)

The Val function converts the numbers in a string into a value. If the string contains any non-numeric characters, then only that portion of the string before the first non-numeric character is converted. Val will also properly convert a negative sign or exponentiation signs (see Chapter 4).

The *Val* Function

The format of Val is

```
Val(string)
```

This function converts the leading numbers in *string* into a number.

Example

```
Num = Val("12345abcde")
```

When this code is executed, Num will contain the value 12345.

Converting a Number to a String. Many times you will want to convert a number to a string. The Str$ function allows you to do the opposite of the Val function. It converts a number into a string, adding a sign placeholder at the beginning (a space if the number is positive or a minus sign if the number is negative).

The *Str$* Function

The format of Str$ is

```
Str(number)
```

This function converts *number* into a string.

Example

```
OrigNum = 9876
NumOut$ = Str$(OrigNum)
```

When this code is executed, NumOut$ will contain the characters " 9876". Notice the leading space, which is a placeholder for a negative sign.

Creating Strings

Occasionally you will need a string of characters that are all the same. For example, you may be printing a report and need a line of dashes across the page. There are many ways to generate a string of some number of a specific character, but the built-in Visual Basic functions, Space and String, are the easiest.

Making a String of Characters. Suppose you needed that string of dashes and your page was 80 characters wide. The following code returns a string consisting of exactly 80 dashes:

```
DashString$ = String$(80,"-")
```

The *String$* Function
The format of String$ is

```
String$(number, string)
```

This function returns a string exactly *number* characters long, made up of *string*.

Example

```
AString$ = String$(5, "A")
```

Returns the string "AAAAA".

Note

While you can pass a string containing more than one character, String will use only the first character of the string. For example, String$(5, "ABC") returns "AAAAA" not "ABCABCABCABCABC".

Making a String of Spaces. Often the character you need is the space, so there is a special function just for generating strings comprised of only spaces—Space.

The string you get using Space is no different than the string you get using String with a space character. If you prefer, you can always use the String function and forget about Space.

The *Space* Function

The format of Space is

     Space(*number*)

This function returns a string consisting of *number* spaces.

Example

     SpaceString$ = Space(10)

Returns a string consisting of 10 space characters.

Other String Functions

So far you have learned that Visual Basic provides quite a few different string functions. You have not learned them all, however. Visual Basic also provides other functions that allow you to do things like determine the length of a string, determine if one string is contained within another, and extract different parts of a string.

Finding the Length of a String.

The *Len* Function

The format of Len is

     Len(string)

This function returns an integer count of the number of characters in string.

Example

     Dim CharCount As Integer
     CharCount = Len("How many here?")

Returns 14. (Don't forget to count the spaces as characters.)

Strings Within Strings.

The *InStr* Function

The format of InStr is

```
InStr([start,] string1, string2)
```

This function returns a Variant that is the position of the first occurrence of *string2* in *string1*. If specified, *start* is the first position in *string1* at which time *InStr* begins searching for a match.

Example

```
Dim FoundAt As Variant
FoundAt = InStr("Where is found at found at?",
➥"found at")
```

FoundAt contains the number 10, which is the character position of the first occurrence of the phrase "found at".

Extracting the Ends of a String. If you only require the leftmost or rightmost portions of a word, then the Left$ and Right$ functions are the most convenient. All you need to do is tell Visual Basic how many characters to strip from the string.

The *Left$* and *Right$* Functions

The format of the Left$ and Right$ functions is

```
Left(string, number)
Right$(string, number)
```

These functions return a string consisting of either the leftmost (Left$) or rightmost (Right$) *number* characters of *string*.

Examples

```
ResString$ = Left$("The left eight", 8)
```

When this is executed, ResString$ will equal the characters "The left".

```
ResString$ = Right$("The 20 rightmost characters",20)
```

When this is executed, ResString$ will equal the characters "The 20 rightmost cha".

Extracting the Middle of a String. Mid$ is used to return (or extract) any portion of a larger string. You pass Mid$ the starting point in the larger string where you want to begin extracting, as well as how many characters to take from that point forward. If you don't specify the number of characters to take, Mid$ returns the rest of the string.

The *Mid$* Function

The format of Mid$ is

```
Mid$(string, start[, length])
```

Where *string* is the string from which you will extract characters, *start* is the position within that string at which extraction will begin and *length* is the number of characters which will be extracted.

Example

```
Center$ = Mid$("Extract the center of this", 13, 6)
```

When this code is executed, Center$ will equal the characters "center".

Math Functions

Mathematics is an important part of everyday life. You do simple math hundreds of times each day. You buy things and count your change, you calculate the mileage your new car is getting, and many many more things involving simple math.

Sometimes the math you must do is a little more complex. If you're buying a house, you'll need more advanced functions to determine what your payments will be, given a particular interest rate, amount borrowed, and loan duration. If you are a scientist, engineer, or machinist, or you have one of many occupations which require the use of more advanced functions, you will appreciate the power inherent in Visual Basic's math functions.

If you think math is too difficult or you don't have a practical use for it, consider some of the examples you are about to see. Everyone uses math to make life easier, and Visual Basic provides you with the functions to perform that math more quickly and accurately.

Extracting an Integer

If you are just interested in the portion of a number to the left of the decimal point, Int will return it for you.

The *Int* Function

The format of Int is

    Int(*number*)

Where *number* is any numeric value.

Example

    Dim IntegerPortion As Integer
    IntegerPortion = Int(52.94387)

When this code is executed, IntegerPortion contains the value 52.

What if you're interested in only the decimal portion? Simple. Just subtract the Int part from the original number. The decimal portion remains.

Generating Random Numbers

Have you ever played a computer game where the computer deals cards, throws dice, or spins a roulette wheel? Did you ever wonder how the random outcome of those events was simulated? Using Visual Basic's Rnd function, you can easily generate random events.

Before using the Rnd function, you must understand that the random numbers generated by Visual Basic are not truly random. This is why you may hear them referred to as *pseudo-random* numbers. A complete discussion of random numbers and the theory behind generating them would require a book at least as large as this one.

So, if you build a game of chance based on the random number generator in Visual Basic and then develop a system which consistently beats your game, don't take your life savings to Las Vegas—their games generate far more random numbers.

The *Rnd* Function

The format of Rnd is

```
Rnd[(number)]
```

Rnd returns a single-precision number equal to or greater than 0, and less than 1. If the optional number is included, it affects Rnd in the following way:

Number	Result
<0	Same random number is returned every time
0	The number returned last time Rnd was used
>0	The next random number

Example

```
Dim HelterSkelter As Single
HelterSkelter = Rnd
```

When this is run, `HelterSkelter` will contain a random single-precision value.

Something to be aware of when using Visual Basic's random number generator is that each time the program is run, under ordinary circumstances the same series of numbers will be generated. To ensure a different set of numbers, use the `Randomize` statement.

Typically, `Randomize` is issued when your program is started, although it doesn't hurt to issue it as many times as you want.

The *Randomize* Function

The format of Randomize is

```
Randomize
```

Randomize reseeds the random number generator resulting in a different sequence of numbers each time your program is run.

Example

```
Randomize
```

Tip

To generate random integers within a specific range, use the following formula: Int((*biggest* - *smallest* + 1) * Rnd + *smallest*) Where *biggest* is the largest integer you want returned and *smallest* is the lowest integer you want.

Determining the Sign of a Number

When performing mathematical operations, it is sometimes necessary to know the sign of a number, or whether it is equal to zero. For example, before dividing a number by a variable, it is good to know whether that variable is equal to zero. If it is, then the result of the division will be indeterminate and shouldn't be performed because an error would be generated in your program. If you are about to take an even root of a number, you will most likely want to know if that number is negative.

The Sgn function determines whether a number is equal to zero or greater than or less than zero all in one step. This is better than first testing the value to see if it is equal to zero and then testing to see if it was greater than zero or less than zero. The Sgn function is faster and more compact. One real purpose of the Sgn function is to determine whether a value is negative before textually formatting it.

The *Sgn* Function

The format of Sgn is

  Sgn(*number*)

If the *number* is equal to 0, Sgn returns 0. If the number is less than 0, Sgn returns –1. If the number is greater than 0, Sgn returns 1.

Example

  `ResultVal = Sgn(-3)`

When this is run, `ResultVal` will contain the value –1 because the number (–3) is less than 0.

Positive Values

In some calculations, such as square roots, negative numbers are not acceptable (unless you are prepared to write special and highly complex routines for handling imaginary numbers). Sometimes the calculation can continue by ensuring the number is positive. You could test a number before using it and multiply it by –1 if it was negative, thereby changing its sign, but there is an easier way.

The guaranteed result of the Abs function is a positive number.

The *Abs* Function

The format of Abs is

    Abs(*number*)

This function returns the positive value of *number*. Thus, if *number* was originally negative, it will be changed to positive. If *number* was positive, it will remain unchanged.

Example

    ValidResult = Sqr(Abs(UnknownVariable))

Using the Abs function within the square root function guarantees that an error won't occur if UnknownVariable is negative.

Formatting

Formatting refers to the way in which you alter the looks of the information your program presents. The Format function allows you to easily format values for output. For example, consider the number 3.14159265359. When formatted as currency, it is shown as $3.14. When formatted as a percent, it is displayed as 314.16%. When formatted as a medium time, it gives 03:23 a.m. Formatting puts the number in context.

The *Format* Function

The format of Format is

    Format(*expression*[, *fmt*])

Where *expression* is a numeric or string expression and *fmt* is any of a wide range of different formats that can be applied. (For information on available formats, see either the on-line help or the *Visual Basic Language Reference.*)

Example

    Dividends = 4423.7463
    Text1 = Format(Dividends, "Currency")

In this example, Text1 would display Dividends as $4,423.75.

All the preceding examples use one of the predefined formats. You also can create your own formats.

There are many additional standard and optional formats available in Visual Basic. Refer to on-line help or the *Visual Basic Language Reference* for an extensive list.

Miscellaneous Functions

Two functions don't fit into any of the categories discussed so far. One causes your computer to make a beeping noise and the other helps coordinate program execution.

Sounding Off

Did you ever wish your computer could talk to you? Visual Basic can't make that happen (at least not without some third party software), but it can give you an audible cue. This cue is given when you use the Beep statement.

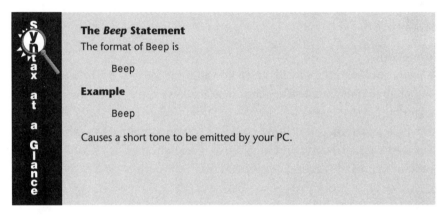

The *Beep* Statement

The format of Beep is

```
Beep
```

Example

```
Beep
```

Causes a short tone to be emitted by your PC.

You can increase the length of the tone by issuing Beep a number of times as in Listing 5.7.

Listing 5.7 Generating longer beeps.

```
For BeepCounter = 1 to 100
   Beep
Next BeepCounter
```

While the Beep command provides no direct means for controlling the frequency of the tone it issues, you can exercise a little control as shown in Listing 5.8.

Listing 5.8 Controlling beep frequency.

```
For BeepDuration = 1 To 100
   Beep
   For BeepPause = 1 To 1000
   Next BeepPause
Next BeepDuration
```

The sound of a single Beep command depends on your system and may vary if run on a different computer. As a result, the sound made by these code snippets also will vary.

Cooperating with Windows

With Windows, you can run more than one program at the same time. Well, almost at the same time. Actually each program takes a turn using the computer's central processing unit, or CPU. Because the CPU executes hundreds of thousands of instructions each second, it can give the appearance of doing many things at once by doing only one thing at a time, but switching quickly between them.

Using the multitasking capabilities of Windows is somewhat like driving. Have you ever tried to pull into heavy traffic from a side street that doesn't have a traffic light? Sometimes you get lucky and another driver will let you in almost immediately. Sometimes those other drivers aren't very cooperative and you wait for a long time.

The programs you run under Windows operate in a similar fashion. They must cooperate with one another in sharing the CPU, or some programs may have to wait a long time before getting a chance to execute. This is a frustrating experience, especially for those who know that it was an oversight on the part of the programmer.

When using Visual Basic, the mechanism for actively cooperating is DoEvents. By using DoEvents, you're telling Windows to check if any other processes need access to the CPU. If none are waiting, then your program continues execution; if there are waiting processes, Windows pauses your program while the others get a chance to run.

To see the implications of programs without DoEvents, examine this code:

Listing 5.9 Code without *DoEvents*.

```
For CounterOne = 1 to 10000
  For CounterTwo = 1 to 10000
    TempVar = Sin(TempVar)
  Next CounterTwo
Next CounterOne
```

When running, this program gives the appearance that the computer is *locked-up*. What has really happened is that Visual Basic is performing a computationally intensive operation—calculating the sine of a variable 100,000,000 times.

DoEvents

You can use DoEvents as either a statement or a function. The only difference is that the function returns the number of visible forms.

The format of the DoEvents statement is

```
DoEvents
```

The format of the DoEvents function is

```
DoEvents ()
```

Examples

```
DoEvents
```

Yields control of the CPU to Windows so it can perform any waiting tasks. When those tasks are finished, control is returned to Visual Basic.

```
NumberOfVisibleForms = DoEvents ()
```

When executed, NumberOfVisibleForms will equal the number of open windows in your application.

Visual Basic is not letting any other processes, including Windows, access the CPU. Because Windows can't access the CPU, it can't respond to your keystrokes or mouse clicks. Windows will queue up a number of your commands and execute them the next chance it gets, but that could take a while. Running the preceding code on a 66MHz 486 takes about one hour to complete. Upon completion, Windows goes on about its normal business; but during that time, the computer will not respond to your input.

Listing 5.10 shows how to insert DoEvents so that Windows remains responsive to your commands.

Listing 5.10 Code with *DoEvents*.

```
For CounterOne = 1 to 100000
  For CounterTwo = 1 to 100000
    DoEvents

    ' additional instructions here

  Next CounterTwo
Next CounterOne
```

When used this way, the DoEvents statement will allow other programs a chance to execute while your program is running.

DoEvents aren't free. They are somewhat costly with respect to time. In Listing 5.10, the DoEvents statement takes about four times as long to execute as the Sin function. Most loops, however, consist of more than just a single function call, so the ratio of time spent on productive work versus the time spent on DoEvents will be greater. Besides, even if it takes somewhat longer to execute your code you can be doing something else in the meantime, instead of just sitting and watching an unresponsive system.

The DoEvents statement costs time because when called, Windows must spend some time seeing if any other processes want to use the CPU. If you use DoEvents every time through a looping process, the aggregate time can be quite high. One solution is to call DoEvents less frequently. By moving the DoEvents call into an outer loop, as shown in Listing 5.11, it is called 100,000 times less frequently. This is still frequent enough to allow some other processing to occur if needed, but not so infrequent as to give the appearance of the system being locked up.

Listing 5.11 Better placement of *DoEvents*.

```
For CounterOne = 1 to 100000
  DoEvents
  For CounterTwo = 1 to 100000

    ' additional instructions here

  Next CounterTwo
Next CounterOne
```

The most useful place for the insertion of DoEvents is inside time-intensive loops.

DoEvents isn't the only way in which Visual Basic yields to Windows. On its own, Visual Basic will occasionally give Windows an opportunity to run, but DoEvents is the easiest way for you to ensure Windows has an opportunity to perform other work.

Using DoEvents in your Visual Basic programs will provide the same feeling you get when someone is kind enough to stop and let you into the flow of traffic.

From Here...

In this chapter, you have sampled the wide variety of functions which make Visual Basic so powerful. You learned the following:

- The benefits of using functions in your programs.

- How to use functions in relation to dates and times.

- How to compare, convert, and create strings using functions.

- How to manipulate strings with functions.

- What common math functions are available.

- How to create notification sounds with your program.

- How to cooperate with other Windows programs.

Chapter 6

Controlling Program Flow

The real strength of the computer is not in its number crunching ability as much as its ability to make decisions.

Visual Basic steps through your program code one line at a time. In this sense, VB follows the path you pave through your code. Decisions based on the comparison of two or more items allow your program to follow one path or another. The potential to pick execution paths is really what makes computers useful. Without this capability, a computer would just be an overgrown hand-held calculator.

Visual Basic provides many ways for you to control how a program is executed. This chapter explores these flow control statements and explains where each is appropriate.

Conditional Execution

In Chapter 5, you learned about comparison operators and how to use them in a program. One of the most common places where they are used is in *conditional statements*. These are programming statements that affect program execution based on the outcome of some sort of logical comparison. These types of statements are very fundamental to any programming language, and Visual Basic is no exception.

There are four types of conditional statements in Visual Basic. They are the If...Then statement, the Select Case structure, and the Do...Loop clause, and the `While...Wend` clause. The following sections explain each of these statements.

If...Then

If the phone rings, answer it. If the dog barks, call me. If I have enough, I'll buy lunch; otherwise, you can. We use a form of `If...Then` statements daily. In common use, we just leave out all the words for a completely formed `If...Then` clause, or we substitute other words with similar meaning.

Take a closer look at the sentences in the preceding paragraph. They are rewritten here in a more structured manner:

```
If the phone rings Then
    answer the phone.

If the dog barks Then
    call me.

If I have enough money Then
    I'll pay for lunch
Else
    you pay for lunch.
```

These examples look very much like the Visual Basic syntax for the `If...Then` statement because making decisions with VB is much like making the simple decisions you make every day. For this reason, `If...Then` statements will feel very natural.

Syntax at a Glance

The If...Then Statement

The format of the If...Then statement is

```
If condition(s) Then instruction
```

or

```
If condition(s) Then
    [instruction(s)]
[ElseIf condition(s) Then
    [instruction(s)]]
[Else
    [instruction(s)]]
End If
```

When used without the optional ElseIf and Else clauses, the instructions between If and End If are executed if the condition(s) evaluated are True.

When used with the `ElseIf...Then` clause, the instructions between `If` and `ElseIf` are executed when the condition(s) following the `If` statement are `True`. If they are `False`, however, the condition(s) after the `ElseIf` statement are evaluated. If the second condition evaluates `True`, the instructions between `ElseIf` and `EndIf` (or the next `ElseIf`) are executed.

The instructions between `Else` and `End If` are executed only when all the initial `If...Then` condition(s) are `False`.

Examples

```
If Age < 13 Then Person = "Child"

If (Age > 13) AND (Age < 20) Then Person = "Adult"

If Age > 20 Then
        Person = "Adult"
        Beep
End If

If Sex = "F" Then
        Type = "Female"
Else
        Type = "Male"
End If
```

Formatting *If...Then* Structures. You should perform only the simplest of tasks with an `If...Then` statement on a single line. It is easier to pick out the statements that will be executed if you use the multiline form. Besides, your code will often grow in complexity as you add functionality to your programs, ultimately requiring the use of the multiline form anyway. There is another disadvantage to the single line form which you will see in Chapter 9, "Debugging."

Notice the indentation of the instructions that will be conditionally executed. This makes the code more readable. It also helps solve the problem of forgetting to put an `End If` at the end of the `If` clause. When the executed statements are indented, you can easily see if you have forgotten the `End If`.

Tip

You can type **endif** at the end of an `If...Then` clause. Visual Basic will automatically convert it to End If.

Caution

Make certain you match an `End If` to every `If` statement. If you forget to do this, Visual Basic will generate an error when you attempt to run the program.

Indentation is especially helpful with nested If clauses. You use a nested If clause when you must make multiple levels of decisions. Listing 6.1 shows an example of nested Ifs.

Listing 6.1 Nested *Ifs*.

```
If X < 25 Then
    If X\2 <> 0 Then
        If X\3 <> 0 Then
            Print "X is prime."
        End If
    End If
End If
```

At first glance, this example doesn't seem to offer any advantage over the code of Listing 6.2.

Listing 6.2 A similar version.

```
If (X < 25) And (X\2 <> 0) And (X\3 <> 0) Then
    Print "X is prime."
End If
```

There are advantages, however, in nesting the If...Then structures. For instance, consider the example shown in Listing 6.3.

Listing 6.3 Nested *Ifs* with additional code.

```
If X < 25 Then
    Print "Likelihood X prime is 10/24"
    If X\2 <> 0 Then
        Print "Likelihood X prime is now 10/13"
        If X\3 <> 0 Then
            Print "X is prime."
        End If
    End If
End If
```

The nested If gives you the opportunity to do additional work between checking each condition.

Notice that in Listing 6.2, the conditions appear in parentheses. The parentheses help prevent confusion over which operations will be executed first. Using parentheses never hurts; in fact, they are recommended for the sake of clarity.

Using *Not* With *If...Then*. The use of Not can sometimes make an If statement more readable, as shown in Listings 6.4 and 6.5.

Listing 6.4 *If* without *Not*.

```
Home = True

    ' instructions

If Home = False Then
    Print "No one here!"
End If
```

Listing 6.5 *If* with *Not*.

```
Home = True

    ' instructions

If Not Home Then
    Print "No one here!"
End If
```

The code in Listing 6.4 works the same as the code in Listing 6.5 because conditions always evaluate to True or False. As discussed in Chapter 4, Not negates, or switches, the logical condition of an expression—thus, Not True equals False and Not False equals True. If you plan the names of your variables and what they contain, your code can be much easier to read. Code that is easy to read allows you to concentrate on solving the problem at hand; it also is easier for others to understand.

Select Case

Many of the problems encountered while programming require long and often complicated If...Then statements. For example, the code of Listing 6.6 is required to determine which digit (1 to 5) a single digit number is. This code would be twice as long if checking for ten digits. It would be almost five times as long if checking for every character of the alphabet.

Listing 6.6 *If...Then* code to determine a digit from 1 to 5.

```
If Digit = 1 Then
  Print "One"
ElseIf Digit = 2 Then
  Print "Two"
ElseIf Digit = 3 Then
  Print "Three"
ElseIf Digit = 4 Then
  Print "Four"
ElseIf Digit = 5 Then
  Print "Five"
End If
```

One of the most convenient program flow constructs is the `Select Case` statement, which you can use to get rid of a long series of `If...Then` conditions. It is easy to use and provides a good solution to a wide variety of problems.

The *Select Case* Statement

The format of the Select Case statement is

```
Select Case testexpression
    [Case expression
        [instructions]]
    [Case expression
        [instructions]]
    [Case Else
        [instructions]]
End Select
```

Where `testexpression` is any numeric or string expression. If `expression`, in one of the Case clauses, matches the `testexpression`, then the statements associated with that Case clause, and only the statements associated with that Case clause, are executed.

Expression can take one of four forms.

- A numeric or string expression such as `Val(NumberString)` or `Front$`.

- An explicit value such as 3 or True.

- A range of values by using the `To` keyword as in `A To Z` or `5 To 9`.

- A conditional range of values by using the `Is` keyword such as `Is < 0` or `Is <> 0`.

Examples

```
Select Case Age
    Case Is < 13
        Person = "Child"
    Case Is <20
        Person = "Teenager"
    Case Is >= 20
        Person = "Adult"
        Beep
End Select

Select Case Sex
    Case "F"
        Type = "Female"
    Case "M"
        Type = "Male"
    Case Else
        MsgBox "There's a problem here!"
End Case
```

The code of Listing 6.7 is much shorter, accomplishes the same thing, and is more readable (thus, more reliable) than the code in Listing 6.6.

Listing 6.7 Checking for a digit with *Select Case*.

```
Select Case Digit
    Case 1
        Print "One"
    Case 2
        Print "Two"
    Case 3
        Print "Three"
    Case 4
        Print "Four"
    Case 5
        Print "Five"
End Select
```

> **Note**
>
> You cannot place instructions between the Select Case statement and the first Case clause; it will generate an error when you try to run your program. Place any code you may consider putting here outside the Select Case structure.

When using the Select Case statement, it is good practice to account for all anticipated cases with specific Case clauses and use the Case Else clause to flag an error if an unexpected value is encountered. If you use the Else clause to handle expected values, Visual Basic will process any unexpected values possibly leading to erroneous results or unanticipated errors.

Tip
You can type **Case < "A"** and Visual Basic will automatically convert it to the proper form: Case Is < "A".

Switch

The Select Case statement allows only one test expression, and all the Cases must be related to that single test expression. Switch is different in that you can test different test expressions within the same function.

Visual Basic evaluates the test expressions from left to right. When VB encounters the first True test expression, it doesn't evaluate any further. This behavior is illustrated in Listing 6.8.

Listing 6.8 Evaluation sequence of *Switch*.

```
ResultString = Switch(Dog > Cat, "Woof", Cat > Mouse, "Meow", True,
➥"Problem")
```

> **Note**
>
> The maximum number of options for the Switch function is seven.

The *Switch* Function

The format of the Switch function is

    Switch(exp1, var1 [, exp2, var2 ... [, exp7, var7]])

Where *exp1* through *exp7* are the expressions to evaluate, and *var1*
through *var7* are the values or string contents that will be returned if
the expression evaluated is True.

Example

```
Label1 = "Operation is " & Switch(OpVal = "+",
➥"Addition", OpVal = "-", "Subtraction", OpVal = "*",
➥"Multiplication",OpVal = "/", "Division")
```

Table 6.1 shows the results of the Switch statement in Listing 6.8. Remember
that when a True expression is encountered, Switch stops.

Table 6.1 The results of the *Switch* statement in Listing 6.8

Dog	Cat	Mouse	ResultString
2	1	0	"Woof"
1	2	1	"Meow"
0	1	2	"Problem"

If none of the expressions in the Switch function are True, then no action is
taken. This can cause problems later in your program. Because tracking down
errors is difficult, you should take every conceivable precaution.

Did you notice that the last condition in the Switch function shown in Listing 6.8 is always True? To catch any possible errors in expected values, place a
statement at the end of the switch that always evaluates True, as was done
with the True keyword in this listing.

Looping Structures

Besides conditional statements, Visual Basic also includes several different
types of structures, or constructs, which allow you to repeatedly execute

segments of code as long as certain conditions are met. These types of constructs are one of the reasons that high-level languages are so powerful.

For looping structures, Visual Basic provides the following:

- `While...Wend`

- `Do...Loop`

- `For...Next`

By effectively using these three types of constructs, you can create tight, concise code that still accomplishes a great deal of work. The following sections describe each of these constructs.

While...Wend

If you must perform an action over and over until some condition is met, but you don't know how many times it must be done beforehand, you can use a `While...Wend` loop.

In execution, a `While...Wend` loop is identical to a `Do While` version of a `Do...Loop`, as described in the following section. One advantage of `While...Wend`, however, is that it is syntactically the same construct as is used in several other high-level languages. This makes it more comfortable to use for some people who are new to Visual Basic.

The *While...Wend* Statement

The format of the `While...Wend` statement is

```
While condition
    [Instruction(s)]
Wend
```

Where the `condition` is an expression that can be evaluated to a `True` or `False` value. The instructions between the `While` and `Wend` are repeated until the condition becomes `False`.

Examples

```
Response$ = ""
GetResponse                 'Execute user input
While Response$ <> "Exit"
    ProcessRecord           'Call subroutine to process
                            ➥it all
    GetResponse             'Call subroutine to get
                            ➥more user input
Wend
```

Do...Loop

A newer Visual Basic looping construct is the `Do...Loop`. In some instances it is very much like the `While...Wend` loop described in the previous section. It is, however, much more versatile and capable.

A `Do...Loop` allows you to check a condition and then execute a block of code if that condition is met. If the condition isn't met, the block of code is skipped over.

By using the `Do Until` version of the `Do...Loop`, you check the condition at the end of the block of code.

The *Do...Loop* Statement

The format of the Do...Loop statement is

```
Do [{While ¦ Until} condition]
    [Instruction(s)]
    [Exit Do]
    [Instruction(s)]
Loop
```

or

```
Do
    [Instruction(s)]
    [Exit Do]
    [Instruction(s)]
Loop [{While ¦ Until} condition]
```

If you include *condition*, then you must use either the While or the Until keyword.

The `Exit Do` statement allows you to abort the loop before the Exit condition is met. This is useful if you test a second condition within the loop.

Examples

```
CounterValue = 0
Do While CounterValue < 10
    Print CounterValue
    CounterValue = CounterValue + 2
Loop

CounterValue = 0
Do
    Print CounterValue
    Countervalue = CounterValue + 2
Loop While CounterValue < 10
```

Both of these examples, when executed, print the numbers 0, 2, 4, 6, and 8.

The First Time Through. Given any task utilizing a `Do...Loop`, there are usually several ways to accomplish it. You can use a `Do While...Loop` or a `Do...Loop While`, or you can use a `Do Until...Loop` or a `Do...Loop Until`.

Most of the time, you can select the `Do...Loop` version that you are most comfortable with and that reads most smoothly. You must be aware of one problem, which is exemplified by Listing 6.9.

Listing 6.9 One version of a *Do...Loop*.

```
Do
    MsgBox "X=" & Str$(X) & "    Y=" & Str$(Y)
    X = X + IncValue
Loop While X < Y
```

This is a very simple program. If your intent in creating the loop is to print the message box only when X is less than Y, then your logic has failed you. This loop will *always* execute at least once. Instead, use an alternate form of the `Do...Loop`, as shown in Listing 6.10.

Listing 6.10 A better version of a *Do...Loop*.

```
Do While X < Y
    MsgBox "X=" & Str$(X) & "    Y=" & Str$(Y)
    X = X + IncValue
Loop
```

In this case, the test is done *before* the loop is entered the first time, and it is never executed if the test fails (when X is less than Y).

Exiting a Loop. If you use an `Exit Do` in the inner `Do...Loop` of a nested set of `Do...Loop`s, it will return control to the structure one level above. In Listing 6.11, when the `Exit Do` statement is encountered, the next line to be executed is the last `Loop` statement.

Listing 6.11 Use of *Exit Do*.

```
Do While Not EOF(FileHandle)
    Input #FileHandle, CharBuffer
    Do While Len(CharBuffer) > 0
        ThisChar = Left(CharBuffer,1)
        CharBuffer = Right(CharBuffer, Len(CharBuffer) - 1)
        If ThisChar = "X" Then
            MsgBox "Found an X in this line"
            Exit Do
        End If
    Loop
Loop
```

Notice the use of Not in the initial Do statement—again for readability. You must not overestimate the importance of making your code easy to follow. A good programmer's source code reads like a story.

For...Next

For...Next is a compact way to execute a set of instructions a certain number of times. You can use Do...Loop and a counter variable, but For...Next is more convenient.

The *For...Next* Statement

The format of the For...Next statement is

```
For counter = startval to endval [Step incrval]
    [Instruction(s)]
    [Exit For]
    [Instruction(s)]
Next[ counter]
```

Where *counter* is the loop counter, *startval* is the value the loop starts counting at, *endval* is the value at which the loop stops executing, and *incrval* is an optional value by which the counter will be incremented each time through the loop.

Examples

```
Full$ = ""
For LoopCounter = 1 To 10
    Full$ = Full$ & " " & Chr$(64 + LoopCounter)
Next LoopCounter
```

When this code has executed, Full$ will be equal to "A B C D E F G H I J".

The code in Listings 6.12 and 6.13 show equivalent versions of the For...Next loop and the Do...Loop construct. Once again, using the right program-flow control structure for the job leads to more compact, readable code.

Listing 6.12 Simple *For...Next*.

```
For LoopCounter = 1 To 10
    Print "Pass" & Str$(LoopCounter)
Next LoopCounter
```

Listing 6.13 Equivalent *Do...Loop*.

```
LoopCounter = 1
Do While LoopCounter <= 10
   Print "Pass" & Str$(LoopCounter)
   LoopCounter = LoopCounter + 1
Loop
```

Incrementing the Loop Counter. Within a `For...Next` loop the instructions are always executed before the loop counter is incremented. If the increment causes the loop counter value to exceed the ending value, then the loop is exited. Otherwise it is executed again.

While it is possible to modify the value of a loop counter in a `For...Next` loop, it can make following the execution of code difficult. Try to structure your code so this isn't necessary.

If you don't specify a `Step` value, then the loop counter is incremented by 1 each time through the loop. Specifying a negative step value causes the loop counter to be decremented. Listing 6.14 demonstrates an example of counting backwards using a negative increment for the loop counter.

Listing 6.14 A negative increment.

```
Full$ = ""
For LoopCounter = 10 To 5 Step -1
   Full$ = Full$ & Chr$(64 + LoopCounter)
Next LoopCounter
```

When this code has completed execution, `Full$` will contain the string `JIHGFE`.

> **Note**
>
> Always make sure the ending value is greater than the starting value when a positive `Step` value is used or implied (as it is when you leave the `Step` value off).
>
> If the starting value is greater than the ending value, Visual Basic will never execute the code in the loop unless you are using a negative `Step` value.

The loop test is not actually for equality, which can lead to potential problems. The code in Listing 6.15 will result in the message dialog box displaying the values 1,4,7, and 10. The values contained in LoopCounter through the loop are 1,4,7,10 and finally, 13. The For...Next loop compares 13 to the

Tip

It is entirely possible to omit the counter name after the `Next` keyword in a `For...Next` loop. Try to resist the temptation to do this, however. Using the variable name helps to match the `Next` with its `For` when you have multiple or nested `For...Next` loops.

ending value of 12 and because 13 is larger than 12, the loop terminates. If a For...Next loop required an exact match on the final pass, it can enter an endless loop where the condition necessary for its termination was never met.

Listing 6.15 *For...Step...Next.*

```
For LoopCounter = 1 To 12 Step 3
    MsgBox LoopCounter
Next LoopCounter%
```

> ### Note
>
> With a positive `Step` value, the loop terminates when the counter is greater than the end value. If the `Step` value is negative, then the loop terminates when the counter is less than the end count. For example, consider the following line of code:
>
> ```
> For LoopCount = 1 To 13 Step 3
> ```
>
> This loop terminates when LoopCount is 16 because 16 > 13. However,
>
> ```
> For LoopCount = 12 To 1 Step -3
> ```
>
> terminates when LoopCount is 0 because 0 < 1.

Nesting a *For...Next* Loop. For...Next statements can be nested. This has certain advantages over a single For...Next loop. Listing 6.16 shows a For...Next loop with a large terminal count.

Tip
The total number of times the statements in the inner loop of a nested For...Next structure will execute is equal to the product of all the individual For...Next loop iterations.

Listing 6.16 *For...Next* with large terminal count.

```
LoopTotal = 0
For Counter = 1 to 100000000
    LoopTotal = LoopTotal + Counter
Next Counter
```

One disadvantage to the code of Listing 6.16 is that while it is running, Visual Basic never yields control to any other waiting programs. Listing 6.17 terminates after the same number of iterations as Listing 6.16, but affords the opportunity to insert a few DoEvents commands to give Windows a chance to attend to any housekeeping. (The DoEvents statement is covered in Chapter 5.)

Listing 6.17 Breaking up a large *For...Next*.

```
LoopTotal = 0
For CounterOuter = 1 to 10000
    For CounterInner = 1 to 10000
        LoopTotal = LoopTotal + Counter
    Next CounterInner
    DoEvents
Next CounterOuter
```

GoTo

You may have heard many bad things about GoTo. In the early days of BASIC, before the more structured flow control statements you saw earlier in this chapter were available, GoTo was the easiest way to control program flow. This led to unmanageable code, sometimes called *spaghetti code* because of its similarity to a plate full of snarled spaghetti.

The *GoTo* Statement

The format of the GoTo statement is

```
GoTo {label ¦ linenumber}
```

You must use either a program label or a line number with the GoTo statement. (Most of the time you will use the former; the latter is for compatibility with older versions of BASIC.) The label or line number must be within the same procedure as the GoTo statement.

Example

```
GoTo TheEnd
```

While it has been proven that it is never necessary to use a GoTo, it is sometimes convenient to do so. If you don't go overboard with GoTos, their occasional use, in situations that are difficult to solve with other flow control constructs, is considered acceptable programming practice.

Any time you are about to use a GoTo statement, take a few moments to consider whether one of the other program flow constructs can do the job in a more readable fashion. While you may have a good grasp of the overall flow within your program while you are writing it, when you come back to it in a year it will take a while to remember what you were doing. Too many GoTos can make it take far longer.

The use of a label in conjunction with a GoTo is more descriptive than using a number. Compare Listings 6.18 and 6.19, and you will see that Listing 6.19 is easier to read.

Listing 6.18 *GoTo* with a line number.

```
10 StopNow = False
...
130 ...
140 If StopNow Then Goto 999
...
999 End
```

Listing 6.19 *GoTo* with a label.

```
StopNow = False
...
If StopNow Then Goto Finished
...
Finished:
End
```

> **Note**
>
> GoTos can only transfer control to a line within the procedure in which they appear.

From Here...

This chapter provided a description of some of the most powerful instructions available within Visual Basic. They are powerful because they control the execution path of your code. In this chapter, you learned the following:

- How to use the If...Then structure.

- How a Select Case structure works.

- How the Switch function differs from a Select Case structure.

- There are four versions of the Do...Loop, each applicable to different situations.

- The For...Next loop is used for executing code a set number of times.

- In certain limited situations, you can use the GoTo command to change program flow.

Chapter 7

Using Data Structures

Frequently, when dealing with information, there is a built-in relationship between certain pieces of that information. For example, a book has a title, an ISBN number, a page count, and an author. Each book has a corresponding value for each of these items. Visual Basic has the capability of using data structures so you can better handle related information.

In this chapter, you will learn about data arrays, user-defined data types, and how you can work with these data structures. You will even learn how you can search and sort arrays in your programs.

Understanding Arrays

One of the most fundamental data structures is the *array*. An array is simply an ordered collection of data. Take ten pennies and line them up on the top of a table—you have an array of pennies. For reference purposes, you can just as easily refer to the first penny in the array or the seventh penny in the array. Arrays are just a way of organizing things that have something in common.

Arrays of related items are used frequently in Visual Basic programs. The benefit of arrays is that they enable you to categorize items and concentrate only on the element of the array in which you are interested.

When you have an array of similar elements, such as the array of pennies, you have more than just an ordered collection. You know that most aspects of the pennies are identical. All pennies are made of copper (except for one year during World War II, which we'll ignore for the purpose of this example), and all pennies are of approximately the same diameter, weight, and thickness.

If you collect pennies in the random change you receive each day, there is one thing that is likely to vary from penny to penny—the date of minting. If you were interested in describing your collection of pennies, you may write a list as shown in Table 7.1.

Table 7.1 Array of Penny Years	
Element	**Year**
1	1979
2	1972
3	1994
4	1983
5	1993
6	1991
7	1988
8	1976
9	1959
10	1924

Setting Up an Array

To allocate adequate memory to hold arrays, you must declare the array so that Visual Basic will know how to handle it. One way you can declare the array is to use the Dim statement. Dim tells Visual Basic to set aside the right amount of space for the array.

The *Dim* Statement

When used for setting up arrays, the format of Dim is

```
Dim arrayname([lower To ]upper[, [lower To]
➥upper]...)[As type]
```

Where *arrayname* is the name of the array, *lower* and *upper* are the lower and upper bounds, respectively, of that array dimension, and *type* is the Visual Basic data type of the array member.

Example

```
Dim Pennies(101)
Dim Pennies(1 To 101) As Integer
```

Arrays can also be declared `Global` so they may be accessed in all forms, procedures, and modules of your program.

The *Global* Statement

The format of `Global` is

```
Global arrayname([lower To ]upper[, [lower To]
➥upper]...)[As type]
```

Where *arrayname* is the name of the array, *lower* and *upper* are the lower and upper bounds, respectively, of that array dimension, and *type* is the Visual Basic data type of the array member.

You can only use `Global` in the Declarations section of the startup module, or in an independent global variables module.

Example

```
Global Nickels(5)
Global Nickels(1 To 5) As Integer
```

There is one more way in which you can declare an array. You may have an occasion to use an array within a function or subroutine with the requirement that the contents of the array be retained between procedure calls. In other words, you don't want the array to be reinitialized each time you enter the procedure. In these cases, use the `Static` declaration.

The *Static* Statement

The format of `Static` is

```
Static arrayname([lower To ]upper[, [lower To]
➥upper]...)[As type]
```

Where *arrayname* is the name of the array, *lower* and *upper* are the lower and upper bounds, respectively, of that array dimension, and *type* is the Visual Basic data type of the array member.

`Static` is used in procedures to retain the value of the declared variable(s) between calls to the procedure. Each `Static` variable will retain its value as long as the program is running.

Example

```
Static Dimes(1 To 10) As Integer
```

Changing Arrays on the Fly

Because arrays can consume so much memory it is convenient to change the size of the array as required during run time.

Frequently, you don't know how many dimensions or elements you have until after your program is already running. In these cases, it is also necessary to change the size of the array at run time. The ReDim statement does just that.

The *ReDim* Statement

After a variable has been dimensioned with Dim or Global, you can use ReDim to change the number of elements in the dimensions. The format of ReDim is

```
ReDim [Preserve ]arrayname ([lower To ]upper[,
➥[lower To ]upper]...)[As type]
```

Where *arrayname* is the name of the dynamic array, *lower* and *upper* are the lower and upper bounds, respectively, of that array dimension, and *type* is the data type of the array member.

ReDim reallocates storage space for a previously declared array. The optional Preserve clause causes ReDim to retain the values contained in the array prior to the issue of ReDim. Note that if you use Preserve, you can resize only the last array dimension.

Example

```
ReDim Quarters(5 To 25) As Integer
```

ReDim is used to modify the bounds of an array. In effect, it allows you to dynamically change how your arrays are used while the program is running. You can't use it to change the data type for a variable. For a nondynamic array, you must get rid of the original variable entirely, and then you are free to redimension the variable.

If you want to free the memory space allocated to a dynamic array, use Erase. When you use Erase, you can get rid of the variable altogether.

Multidimensional Arrays

Sometimes there is more than one aspect, or dimension, to an array. In the penny example, if you look closely, you can also find another feature which varies—the letter on the face of the penny representing the mint at which the penny was made. You can add another column to Table 7.1 showing the mint next to the year. You will then have a multidimensional array.

The *Erase* Statement
The format of Erase is

```
Erase arrayname[, arrayname]...
```

Where *arrayname* is the name of the array.

Erase reinitializes the elements of a fixed array, or deallocates memory space assigned to a dynamic array.

Example

```
Erase Pennies, Nickels, Dimes, Quarters
```

Multidimensional arrays are especially useful because they allow you to track and manipulate more than one aspect of the item you have placed into an array. As an example of the usefulness of multidimensional arrays, some of the characteristics of a family have been arranged into an array in Table 7.2. This array shows several aspects of each family member.

Table 7.2 Multidimensional array of family members

Name	Sex	Birthday	Age	Occupation
Sam	M	5/8	27	Engineer
Ginger	F	8/11	24	Teacher
Beth	F	12/24	21	Student
Casey	M	6/13	18	Student

Arrays can consume an enormous amount of space. The amount of space an array requires is approximately equal to the product of the number of elements in the array, times the number of array dimensions, times the number of bytes required for each individual data type.

The family array shown in Table 7.2 has four array elements and five dimensions; so, by the preceding formula, it consumes 5 × 4, or 20 memory locations. If you were dealing with a family of eight, and you tracked only a dozen characteristics of each family member, you would be working with an array that consumed 8 × 12, or 96 memory locations. If you constructed an array that included relatives and friends, well... you get the idea. Arrays can consume a lot of memory.

To represent the family member array in Visual Basic, you must first declare it. Declaring the array sets aside memory space to hold the array elements. You learned how to do this earlier in the chapter, but you cannot use the `Dim` statement (by itself) to define an array for your family. The different elements of the array are of different data types. For example, the Name, Sex, and Occupation elements will be strings, while the age and possibly the date element can be expressed as a number. In this case, traditional arrays are all but useless. Instead, you will need to learn about user-defined data types.

User-Defined Data Types

Although occasionally you may have related information, the data types will vary. You may, perhaps, want to store information on employees in an array. Each employee has a hire date (Date/Time type), a name (String), a wage rate (Currency), and a job class (Integer). How can you use an array to store this information when the data types vary?

To store the employee information, you must first create a *user-defined data type* so all elements of the array can be the same. A user-defined data type "packages" a collection of other data types into an "envelope," which can then be treated as though it were a standard Visual Basic data type.

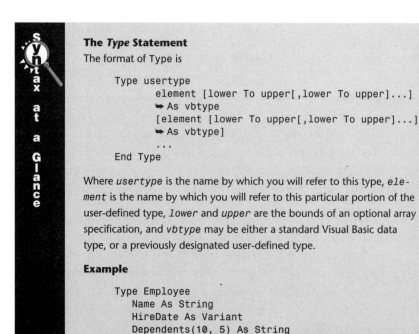

The *Type* Statement
The format of Type is

```
Type usertype
        element [lower To upper[,lower To upper]...]
        ➥ As vbtype
        [element [lower To upper[,lower To upper]...]
        ➥ As vbtype]
        ...
    End Type
```

Where *usertype* is the name by which you will refer to this type, *element* is the name by which you will refer to this particular portion of the user-defined type, *lower* and *upper* are the bounds of an optional array specification, and *vbtype* may be either a standard Visual Basic data type, or a previously designated user-defined type.

Example

```
Type Employee
   Name As String
   HireDate As Variant
   Dependents(10, 5) As String
End Type
```

The Type statement may only appear in a general code module, and you must place the statement in the Declarations section of the code module. This placement ensures you can use the user-defined type throughout that module.

To obtain the value of one of the variables contained in a user-defined type, use the name of the user-defined type variable and then the name of the specific element in that type, separated by a period. Listing 7.1 shows an example.

Listing 7.1 User type declaration and usage.

```
Type Dogs
   Name As String
   Age As Integer
   Breed As String
End Type

Dim PoundDogs(100) As Dogs

PoundDogs(5).Name = "Spot"
PoundDogs(5).Age = 4
PoundDogs(5).Breed = "Scottie"
```

> **Note**
>
> If you declare an array within a user-defined type, you must use an actual number (rather than a variable) to declare its dimensions. You may not declare a dynamic array with a user-defined type.

User-defined data types are used quite frequently with file access, such as when you are working with random-access files. This use of user-defined data types is covered in Chapter 10.

Getting Information About an Array

Arrays are quite flexible. They can have any number of dimensions up to 60 and over 32,000 elements, memory providing. Because arrays are so flexible, you must find their bounds.

> **Note**
>
> Most likely, you will never be able to create an array that has 60 dimensions and/or 32,000 elements. Remember that arrays tend to be memory hogs. The memory in your system will be exhausted long before you reach these limitations.

You can use the LBound and UBound functions to return the smallest and largest subscript of any array dimension.

The *LBound* and *UBound* Functions

The format of LBound and UBound is

```
LBound(array [,dimension])
UBound(array [,dimension])
```

Where *array* is the array name and *dimension* is the dimension of the array for which you want to return the bounds. If dimension is not specified, then 1 is used.

Examples

```
HighEnd = UBound(RPMArray)
NumDim2ArrElements = UBound(Bones, 2) - LBound(Bones,
➡2) + 1
```

Table 7.3 shows the result of various UBound and LBound functions on the array dimensioned in the following code line:

```
Dim TestArray(0 To 5, -2 To 6, -25 To 0)
```

Table 7.3 *UBound* and *LBound* Results

Function Call	Return Value
LBound(TestArray,1)	0
UBound(TestArray,1)	5
LBound(TestArray,2)	–2
UBound(TestArray,2)	6
LBound(TestArray,3)	–25
UBound(TestArray,3)	0

Unfortunately, Visual Basic doesn't have a command that tells us the number of dimensions an array contains. You can, however, create your own function that will do the trick. If you try to access an array dimension that doesn't exist, you will get an error 9, Subscript out of range. You can use this behavior to find the number of dimensions of an array, as shown in Listing 7.2.

Listing 7.2 Function to return the number of array dimensions.

```
Function ArrayDimensions (ArrayOfInterest())
    Dim LoopCounter As Integer, RetVal As Integer
    On Error GoTo ArrayHandler:
    LoopCounter = 2
    Do While True
        RetVal = LBound(ArrayOfInterest, LoopCounter)
        LoopCounter = LoopCounter + 1
    Loop
Exit Function

ArrayHandler:
    Resume ByeBye
    ByeBye:
    ArrayDimensions = LoopCounter - 1
End Function
```

The ArrayDimensions function in Listing 7.2 steps through the dimensions of the array, trying to execute the function LBound on each dimension. If that dimension exists, no error is generated and the next dimension is tried. When LBound is attempted on a nonexistent dimension, an error is generated.

The error handler assigns the value of the highest dimension to ArrayDimensions, the name of the function, so it can be passed back to the line that called ArrayDimensions in the first place. The highest dimension is the one immediately before the one that generated the error, so you must subtract one dimension from the value of LoopCounter that generated the error.

> **Note**
>
> LoopCounter starts at 2 because it isn't necessary to check the first dimension of the array—all arrays have at least one dimension. By considering the possible values for this variable, you save a little execution time. You should always think about the possible values your variables can assume. It helps prevent errors and can often save a great deal of execution time. In this case only a little execution time is saved, but in others, you can save seconds, minutes, or more.

Did you notice the line Do While True, which begins the testing loop? In previous chapters, you learned how to use different logical expressions with Do...While loops. The one common feature is that each of these expressions always evaluates to either True or False. By explicitly placing a True in the Do...While loop, you effectively say "do this forever." But if the loop is executed forever, how do you keep from ending up in an endless loop? You already know that no Visual Basic array has more than 60 dimensions. Eventually, an error is generated and the error handling code terminates the `Do...While` loop.

Note that you also could have used the following code in place of `Do While True:`

```
Do
    RetVal = LBound(ArrayOfInterest, LoopCounter)
    LoopCounter = LoopCounter + 1
Loop
```

This version of the loop will also execute forever. Either usage is just as effective; either one is just as acceptable. It all depends on your programming style.

Listing 7.2 did not show the way the function was called or the way the array was passed. The following code line, however, shows how the function can be called:

```
NumberOfDimensions = ArrayDimensions (ThisArray())
```

Notice the empty parentheses. This informs Visual Basic that an entire array must be passed to the function. You must also include the empty parentheses in the function declaration, as shown earlier in Listing 7.2.

Starting to Count

You normally start counting at one. Computers and computer languages are typically different, however. Visual Basic starts all of its arrays, unless told otherwise, at zero. You don't have to use the zero element if you don't want to; if you do, however, it is available.

Unless you specifically need it, having a zero element in all dimensions of all arrays wastes memory. Use the `Option Base` statement to force Visual Basic to start all array indices from 1 instead of 0, thereby saving valuable memory.

The amount of memory regained depends on the number of dimensions in your arrays. The total memory an array consumes is the product of the number of its dimensions, times the number of elements, multiplied by the number of bytes required for the data type of each element in the array. By reducing the number of elements by one (when you use `Option Base 1`), you reduce the amount of memory needed to hold the array by the number of dimensions in that array. If your application uses arrays with many dimensions or if it uses many arrays, the savings can be significant.

The *Option Base* Statement

The format of `Option Base` is

        Option Base value

Where *value* is either 1 or 0.

Using the `Option Base` statement is optional. If not used, Visual Basic will start all arrays with an index value of 0. If you decide to use `Option Base`, it must be used in the Declarations section of the startup module; it must also be used before declaring any arrays.

Example

        Option Base 1

Note

If an array is declared using the optional To keyword, the array bounds specified with To will override the bounds set by `Option Base`. The optional To keyword in the `Dim`, `Global`, `Static`, and `ReDim` statements provides greater flexibility in the control of array bounds. Its use is recommended.

Searching

Arrays are convenient because they provide an organized manner in which to hold large amounts of related information. Sometimes you will need to find a specific piece of that information—that is, you will have to search the array.

Searching is a relatively easy task to perform. It only requires the use of the `If...Then` and `For...Next` statements, which you learned about in Chapter 6. You can use `For...Next` to step through an array, one element at a time. `If...Then` performs the actual checking for a match. Listing 7.3 is a code listing for searching an array for a value.

Listing 7.3 Searching an array.

```
' Place the following Dim statement in the general declarations
section
Dim ArrayName(20, 20) As String

' Place the following code in a form module
Dim ThisIndex As Integer

FillArray(ArrayName())              'A procedure to populate the array

For ThisIndex = LBound(ArrayName,2) To UBound(ArrayName,2)
    If ArrayName(2) = "Hornblower" Then
        If ArrayName(1) = "Horatio" Then
          MsgBox "Element " & Str(ThisIndex), ,"Found Horatio
          ➡Hornblower!"
        End If
    End If
Next ThisIndex
```

The code of Listing 7.3 steps through each element of the array starting with the first element returned by LBound and finishing with the last element returned by UBound. You use the If statements to first check the LastName element and then, if that matches, the FirstName element.

This example also shows the usefulness of the LBound and UBound functions. These functions allow you to build generic array-handling routines that are not dependent on an exact number of elements. In Listing 7.3, this is assumed to be the case when it comes to the FillArray procedure, which is not shown. ArrayName is passed to the procedure, where it is assumed to be accessed and filled. The FillArray procedure can use the LBound and UBound functions to determine how much of the array must be filled, and then control is returned to the example where the array is searched.

Sorting

Frequently you will need to sort elements in an array. This is because the original order of the array is not always the order in which you may want it. For example, suppose the Personnel Manager wants to view an array of employees based on their hire date. If the array was filled with employees alphabetically by their last name, you will need to sort the elements before the Personnel Manager can properly use the array.

You will need to sort the array based on the hire date. But wait! Should you sort from lowest to highest (ascending) or highest to lowest (descending)?

The order in which you sort will be dictated by the requirements of the problem you are trying to solve. In the personnel example, you'll sort in ascending order.

You can sort data in a variety of ways. Some are easy to implement, some are difficult, some are fast (when executed), and some are slow. There is no single best sorting method. The one you should use depends on the data to be sorted and the amount of effort you want to put into sorting it.

There are several good books that describe various sorting methods and the advantages and disadvantages of each. (A quick visit to a well-stocked computer bookstore will introduce you to these books.) In the following two sections, you will learn about two different methods—a simple substitution sort and QuickSort. You will not delve into sorting theory in this book. (There are, however, entire books written on the topic.) Instead, you will learn two different routines you can put to work in your programs right away.

Substitution Sort

Substitution sorts are simple to code, and they work just fine for a small number of values (less than 100). Listing 7.4 shows an example of a substitution sort algorithm.

Listing 7.4 Using a substitution sort on an array.

```
For OuterLoop = 1 to UBound(Array,2) - 1
   LowerElement = OuterLoop
   For InnerLoop = OuterLoop + 1 To UBound(Array,2)
      If Array(InnerLoop) < Array(LowerElement) Then LowerElement =
InnerLoop
   Next InnerLoop
   If LowerElement <> OuterLoop Then
      HoldValue = Array(OuterLoop)
      Array(OuterLoop) = Array(LowerElement)
      Array(LowerElement) = HoldValue
   End If
Next OuterLoop
```

The code of Listing 7.4 uses two For...Next loops to step through an array. The outer loop steps through from the beginning to the next-to-the-last element. The inner loop is then used to find the lowest remaining element in the array. If one is found, the element is swapped with the element specified by the outer loop. When you finish, the array is in sorted order, and you only had to swap a maximum of one element on each pass through the array.

QuickSort

QuickSort is a good general-purpose sorting routine that is much quicker than other methods (thus, the name QuickSort). It sorts, not by doing successive comparisons of your entire array, but by dividing the array into smaller sections and then sorting each of those sections. Listing 7.5 shows a function you can use in your programs to sort an array using this method.

Listing 7.5 Using QuickSort on an array.

```
SUB QuickSort (Array$())
    Max = UBOUND(Array$())
    DIM Stack(49)
    P=1:Q=Max:Top=0
    Do
        Do While P < Q
            Temp1$=Array$(P)
            I=P
            J=Q+1
            Do
                Do
                    J=J-1
                Loop While Array$(J)>Temp1$
                Do
                    I=I+1
                Loop While Array$(I)<Temp1$ AND I<Max
                IF J>I THEN
                    Temp2$=Array$(I)
                    Array$(I)=Array$(J)
                    Array$(J)=Temp2$
                ELSE
                    Exit Do
                ENDIF
            Loop
            Array$(P)=Array$(J)
            Array$(J)=Temp1$
            IF (J-P)<(Q-J) THEN
                Stack(Top+1)=J+1
                Stack(Top+2)=Q
                Q=J-1
            ELSE
                Stack(Top+1)=P
                Stack(Top+2)=J-1
                P=J+1
            ENDIF
            Top=Top+2
        Loop
        IF Top<>0 THEN
            Q=Stack(Top)
            P=Stack(Top-1)
            Top=Top-2
        ELSE
            Exit Do
        ENDIF
    Loop
END SUB
```

QuickSort is harder to explain than the substitution sort. The program basically uses a tree method, repeatedly dividing the array into smaller sections, and then sorting each of those sections. Pointers to each of the sections are maintained in the Stack array. When this array is empty, the sort will have been completed.

From Here...

This chapter demonstrated several techniques that you can build on in order to provide powerful data structure manipulation. Some of the topics discussed were:

- Different methods used to define an array.

- How to change arrays after they are defined.

- How and why you can use multidimensional arrays.

- How to define your own data types.

- How to get information about the structure of an array.

- A handy function for determining the number of elements in an array dimension.

- Instruct Visual Basic where, by default, to start arrays.

- Methods to search arrays.

- Methods to sort arrays.

Chapter 8

Dialog Boxes

The word *dialog* comes from the Greek and means *to converse*. Dialog boxes are windows that convey information to the user of a program and often allow that user to provide directions back to the computer.

A good example of a dialog box is what you see if you try to exit Visual Basic without first saving your changes. The dialog box shown in figure 8.1 appears. Here you learn what happens next, then you are given the opportunity to respond to the potential action.

Fig. 8.1
An example of a dialog box.

Dialog boxes such as these are an integral part of the Windows environment. You can make them a part of your programs as well. Visual Basic provides several functions and facilities for adding and using dialog boxes in your programs. In this chapter, you will learn about these capabilities, and you will see examples of how they work.

Creating a Message Box

One of the most useful ways in which Windows programs have evolved in their communication with their users is dialog boxes. Before Windows, dialog boxes were the exception rather than the rule. Even today, programs written for many other operating systems often don't employ them.

Using dialog boxes results in cleaner screens because the information to be conveyed or collected doesn't use up valuable space on your screen. You also can use dialog boxes also to help guide a user through a specific problem and provide information at just the right moment.

In Visual Basic you can create your own dialog boxes, as you'll see later in this chapter, but there is an even easier way—by using the MsgBox statement. The MsgBox statement is a flexible means of presenting dialog boxes in which you can change the message, title, and buttons shown; you can even add an optional icon.

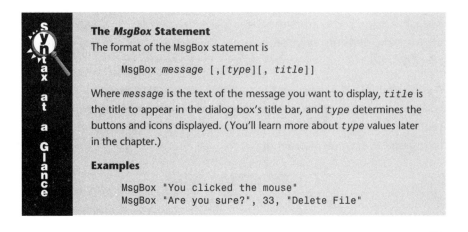

The *MsgBox* Statement

The format of the MsgBox statement is

```
MsgBox message [,[type][, title]]
```

Where *message* is the text of the message you want to display, *title* is the title to appear in the dialog box's title bar, and *type* determines the buttons and icons displayed. (You'll learn more about *type* values later in the chapter.)

Examples

```
MsgBox "You clicked the mouse"
MsgBox "Are you sure?", 33, "Delete File"
```

The Message

The easiest way to use MsgBox is in the form of a statement. All you basically need to do is provide a message you want displayed, and Visual Basic will take care of the rest. The dialog box is displayed, along with an OK button for the user to click, as shown in figure 8.2.

Fig. 8.2

An example of a simple message box.

To try the MsgBox statement on your own, start Visual Basic with a new project. Then add the code in Listing 8.1 to the Form_Click procedure of your form.

Listing 8.1 Your first dialog box.

```
Sub Form_Click ()
    MsgBox "This is My First Dialog Box"
End Sub
```

Run your project and then click the form. You will see the dialog box shown in figure 8.3.

Fig. 8.3
Your first dialog box.

Notice three things about this dialog box. First, the title that appears at the top of the dialog box is the same as the filename you have designated for your project. In the next section, you will learn how to change the title in the dialog box. Second, an OK button appears in the dialog box, and your program is paused until the user clicks the button. This is the only type of button used for the statement form of MsgBox. How you can use different buttons is covered later in this chapter.

The message you used with the MsgBox statement appears in the message box exactly as you entered it. Visual Basic will adjust the size of the dialog box to compensate for whatever text you enter, and it will break lines as necessary. For example, take a look at Listing 8.2, which produced the dialog box shown in figure 8.4.

Listing 8.2 Using a long message with *MsgBox*.

```
Sub Form_Click ()
    MsgBox "This is my second dialog box, and it is much longer than
    ➥the first one. Exactly how long it is depends on when I get
    ➥tired of typing."
End Sub
```

Fig. 8.4
A dialog box with a very long message.

Notice that Visual Basic extended the width of the dialog box and wrapped the text to two lines. If you don't like how VB splits the message over the additional lines, you can control it by adding ASCII line feed characters in your string where you want the message wrapped. An example of formatting the message in this manner is shown in Listing 8.3, with the result shown in figure 8.5.

Listing 8.3 A long message with line breaks inserted.

```
Sub Form_Click ()
    M$ = "This is my third dialog box, and"
    M$ = M$ + Chr$(10) + "it is formatted better than the last one."
    M$ = M$ + Chr$(10) + "Notice how the lines break exactly where"
    M$ = M$ + Chr$(10) + "I think they should."
    MsgBox M$
End Sub
```

Fig. 8.5
A dialog box with a long formatted message.

The Title

MsgBox allows you to change the title of the dialog box as well as the message. You can make this change by simply adding another parameter to the message box statement. Use the code shown in Listing 8.4 to generate a dialog box with a custom title and message.

Listing 8.4 Dialog box with custom title.

```
Sub Form_Click ()
    MsgBox "Ready to Format Your Text",,"Whiz-Bang 2000 Formatter"
End Sub
```

If you take another look back at the syntax of the MsgBox statement, the two commas separating the title from the message are essential. If they are not included, then you will get a Type Mismatch error when you run your program. Normally, a value indicating a type of message box is added between the commas. The next section discusses these values in more detail.

When you run the code shown in Listing 8.4, your dialog box appears as shown in figure 8.6.

Fig. 8.6
An example dialog box showing a custom title.

Icons, Buttons, and Responses

Much of the flexibility of MsgBox is provided through the use of the optional type argument. The second argument to MsgBox determines which icons and buttons are shown in the dialog box.

Changing Icons. Visual Basic allows you to use any of four different icons in your message boxes. These icons are rather standard for Windows dialog boxes; they seem to be used in virtually every program you can think of. Table 8.1 indicates what icons are available, as well as the type value you must use for that icon.

Table 8.1 MsgBox Icon	
Icon	**Value**
Stop Sign	16
Question Mark	32
Exclamation Point	48
i for Information	64

Use the stop sign for serious errors or situations that can cause the loss of data. Use the question mark when obtaining answers to routine questions. The exclamation point is for situations that may have been unexpected by the user, or for emphasis of a message. Use the *i* when presenting a message purely for informational purposes.

As an example, try out the program code shown in Listing 8.5. When you run it, you will see the dialog box shown in figure 8.7.

Listing 8.5 Using an icon with your message box.

```
Sub Form_Click ()
    MsgBox "You just eliminated the national debt.", 64, "Acme
    ➥Problem Solver"
End Sub
```

Fig. 8.7
Using an icon with your message box.

Changing Buttons. Besides allowing you to add icons to your message boxes, Visual Basic allows you to change which buttons are displayed at the bottom of the box. There are seven different buttons that you can use, in six different combinations. Table 8.2 shows the different type values you can use, along with what they represent.

Table 8.2 *MsgBox* Button	
Button(s)	**Value**
OK	0
OK & Cancel	1
Abort, Retry, & Ignore	2
Yes, No, & Cancel	3
Yes & No	4
Retry & Cancel	5

Note

The OK button has a value of 0, which ensures that all dialog boxes have at least one button displayed—the OK button. If you omit the type value in MsgBox, an OK button is displayed by default.

Changing buttons in the dialog box is just as easy as adding icons. As an example, you can use the code in Listing 8.6 to display Yes and No buttons in a dialog box. The result is shown in figure 8.8.

Listing 8.6 Using different buttons in your dialog box.

```
Sub Form_Click ()
    MsgBox "Do you want your program to work?", 4, "Acme Program
    ➥Fixer"
End Sub
```

Fig. 8.8
A dialog box
displaying Yes and
No buttons.

Combining Buttons and Icons. Visual Basic allows you to combine both the icon type values and the button type values so that you can display both icons and different buttons in your dialog boxes. All you need to do is add the two values together.

For example, the value to display a stop sign icon is 16, and the value to display Yes, No, and Cancel buttons is 3. To display them both, you would use a type value of 16 + 3, or 19, in your program. An example of how these values can be used in a program is shown in Listing 8.7, with the result shown in figure 8.9.

Listing 8.7 Using icon and button types together.

```
Sub Form_Click ()
    MsgBox "What should be done with the President?", 32 + 2,
    ➥"Presidential Matters"
End Sub
```

Fig. 8.9
Combining
buttons and icons.

User Feedback. It doesn't usually make sense to change the buttons being displayed in a dialog box if using them has no effect. So far you have done nothing but use the MsgBox statement, which simply displays the message box and then returns to your program. Visual Basic provides a function version of MsgBox that allows you to determine which button the user selected. Based on this information, you can then take the appropriate action.

The *MsgBox* Function
The format of the MsgBox function is

```
    MsgBox(message [,[type][, title]])
```

Where *message* is the text of the message you want to display, *title* is the title to appear in the dialog box's title bar, and *type* determines the buttons and icons displayed.

Examples

```
    YesNo = MsgBox ("Do you want to proceed?", 36,
    ➥"Acquire Information"
    ErrResponse = MsgBox("Cannot determine result", 48 +
    ➥2, "Calculate")
```

You should note that the only difference between the MsgBox statement and function is that the function is used to return a value indicating which button the user pressed.

After the MsgBox function has been invoked and the user has selected a button, the value returned will range from one to seven, and correspond to one of the seven possible buttons listed in Table 8.3.

Table 8.3 Return Values for Selected Buttons	
Value	**Selected Button**
1	OK
2	Cancel
3	Abort
4	Retry
5	Ignore
6	Yes
7	No

You can then make a determination of what to do based on the result. Many times programs will use the Select Case construct (see Chapter 6) to take action after returning from a message box.

Modality

When any of the examples of MsgBox in this chapter are run, you will notice that you cannot select any other form in your Visual Basic project until after you have selected a button on the dialog box. (Although you can select other program windows, you can't select other Visual Basic forms.) This is because VB's MsgBox creates *modal* dialog boxes.

Modality is best explained by example, and you have already seen several good ones in this chapter. Use MsgBox and you have a modal dialog box—one that does not allow you to select any other forms in your current application. Instead, Windows will beep at you if you try to select an "off limits" form.

Modality ensures that you perform certain actions in a specific order. In this case, you must select one of the dialog box buttons before continuing. This particular flavor of modality is termed *application modal* because it only limits your choices within the application. Windows also supports *system modality*.

A system modal dialog box prevents you from taking any action other than selecting one of the dialog box buttons. In this example, you can't even select any other application. The dialog box presented when you attempt to exit Windows is perhaps the best-known example of a system modal dialog box. The next time you exit Windows, try to select something other than a button on that dialog box; you won't be able to.

By default, the MsgBox statement and function support application modality. You can, however, specify system modality by adding the value 4096 to the type value on the program line. This addition makes the message box created by Listing 8.8 a *system modal dialog box*. This means that no other form or application can be selected until the user selects a button from the message box.

Listing 8.8 Creating a system modal dialog box.

```
Sub Form_Click ()
    MsgBox "The Borg are running amok!", 48 + 5 + 4096, "Red Alert"
End Sub
```

When you use MsgBox, there is no way to disable modality. To disable modality, you would need to create a custom dialog box, as discussed later in the chapter.

Getting User Input

A message box is great as long as you need only one of seven answers. What if you need more input? For example, what if you need to know a date to use when aging accounts receivable? In these examples, it is best to use the InputBox$ function. This usage allows you to get a text string from the user, and assign it to a variable.

A dialog box created with the InputBox$ function is application modal—that is, it cannot be changed.

InputBox$ always displays only two buttons—OK and Cancel—as shown in figure 8.10. If the user selects OK (or presses Enter), InputBox$ returns the value that was typed into the text box. If Cancel is selected, a zero-length string ("") is returned.

The *InputBox$* Function

The format of the InputBox$ function is

    InputBox$(*prompt*[, [*title*][, [*default*][, *x*, *y*]]])

Where *prompt* is the text you want to prompt the user with and *title* is the title of the dialog box. *Default* is the initial value placed in the text box. It can be altered by the user. If omitted, the text box will initially be empty. The *x* and *y* values are optional coordinates of where the input box should appear.

Examples

    FirstValue$ = InputBox$("Enter a value")
    PlayerName$ = InputBox$("Type your name", "Player")

Fig. 8.10
An example of
an input box.

Note

You cannot determine, with InputBox$, whether the user selected the Cancel button or the OK button with nothing in the text box. Both actions return a zero-length string.

The Prompt

As with MsgBox, whatever message you use with InputBox$ appears on-screen exactly as you type it. You are limited, however, to messages that are approximately 255 characters long. (Attempting to use a longer message will result in a program error.)

If the message you enter is too long to fit on a single line, Visual Basic will wrap it automatically to the next line. For example, take a look at Listing 8.9, which produced the dialog box shown in figure 8.11.

Listing 8.9 Using a long message with *InputBox$*.

```
Sub Form_Click ()
  . Response$ = InputBox$("Will you please take the time and be kind
    ➥enough to provide your full name so that the installation can
    ➥progress as originally intended?")
End Sub
```

Fig. 8.11
An input box with
a very long
message.

Notice that size of the input box stays the same (see figure 8.10). The only difference is that the user prompt is longer.

If you don't like how Visual Basic splits the message in the dialog box, you can control it by adding ASCII line feed characters in your string where you want the message wrapped. This is shown in Listing 8.10, with the result shown in figure 8.12.

Listing 8.10 Formatting the user prompt.

```
Sub Form_Click ()
  M$ = "To proceed, you need to supply your name. Please do so in
    ➥the following format:"
  M$ = M$ + Chr$(10) + Chr$(10)
  M$ = M$ + "    Doe, John H."
  Response$ = InputBox$(M$)
End Sub
```

Fig. 8.12
A dialog box with
a long formatted
message.

The Title

Normally the InputBox$ function does not display a title in the dialog box. You can, however, display one by adding another parameter to the input box function. Use the code shown in Listing 8.11 to generate a dialog box with a custom title and message, as shown in figure 8.13.

Listing 8.11 Input box with custom title.

```
Sub Form_Click ()
    AgeDate$ = InputBox$("Enter the date for aging accounts",
    ➥"Accounts Receivable")
End Sub
```

Fig. 8.13
An example input
box showing a
custom title.

Default Input

By adding another parameter to the InputBox$ function, Visual Basic allows
you to indicate default text that can be used in your input box. This text
appears in the text box at the bottom of the dialog box, and the user can
accept it by simply pressing Enter. Conversely, if the user starts typing right
away, the default is erased and replaced with whatever the user is typing.

As an example, the code in Listing 8.12 displays the current date as a default
to the prompt. It results in the input box shown in figure 8.14.

Listing 8.12 An input box utilizing a default value.

```
Sub Form_Click ()
    Message$ = " Enter the date for aging accounts:"
    Title$ = "Accounts Receivable"
    AgeDate$ = Date$
    AgeDate$ = InputBox$(Message$, Title$, AgeDate$)
End Sub
```

Fig. 8.14
Default answer
provided in an
input box.

Screen Coordinates

You can locate the dialog box created by InputBox$ at a specific screen location by using the position arguments x and y. Remember that the position is relative to the upper-left corner of the screen and not the form from which InputBox$ is invoked.

If you specify an *x* coordinate, you must also provide a *y* coordinate. The position coordinates are given in twips, which are approximately 1/1440 of an inch. (For an in-depth discussion of twips, see Que's *Using Visual Basic 3*.) If specific screen coordinates are omitted, the dialog box is centered from left to right and appears about one-third down the screen from top to bottom.

Custom Dialog Boxes

Now that you know what a dialog box is and how to use the standard dialog boxes provided by Visual Basic through MsgBox and InputBox$, you can dive right into the creation of a custom dialog box.

Creating the Dialog Box

Figure 8.15 shows the dialog box you'll create—one that collects registration information. Because you want to obtain the name of the individual and the name of the company separately, InputBox$ will not suffice.

Fig. 8.15
A custom dialog box.

First, start Visual Basic and begin work on a brand new form. Then position two labels and two text boxes in the form so that they appear similar to what is shown in figure 8.15. Then make the property changes to the form and other objects as indicated in Table 8.4.

Table 8.4 Object Properties		
Object	**Property**	**Value**
Form	BackColor	&H00C0C0C0&
	BorderStyle	3 – Fixed Double
	Caption	Registration
	ControlBox	False
	MaxButton	False
	MinButton	False
Label1	BackColor	&H00C0C0C0&
	Caption	Your Name
Label2	BackColor	&H00C0C0C0&
	Caption	Your Company
Text1	Text	(delete text)
Text2	Text	(delete text)
Command1	Caption	&OK

The advantages of creating a dialog box in this manner are plentiful. Here are some of the additional features our custom dialog box has over one created with the InputBox$ function:

■ Colored background

■ Two text boxes

■ Underline on the command button

■ Verification code which ensures an entry has been made

If, when creating custom dialog boxes, you add additional buttons, they should be centered across the bottom of the form. This is a Windows standard which, when complied with, will give your programs a familiar look and feel.

If the design of the dialog box is such that command buttons on the bottom don't work well, you may alternatively place them along the right side of the form starting at the top.

Additional Features

There are still a few ways in which you can improve your new dialog box. You can make the OK command button a default button, which means that if the user presses the Enter key, it will be just like selecting the OK button.

To make a default button on the form, change its `Default` property to `True`. Now when the user presses the Enter key, the button will be clicked.

This form doesn't have a Cancel button, but if it did, you may want to set the `Cancel` property of the Cancel button to `True`. When set to `True`, the `Cancel` property for a command button causes that button to be clicked when the Escape key is pressed.

Each form can have only one Default command button and one Cancel command button. You have the option of setting both the `Cancel` and `Default` properties to `True` for a single button. If you do, that command button will be clicked when either the Enter key or Escape key is pressed.

Locating the Dialog Box

If you don't specify a location for your dialog box, it will appear on-screen at the location where it was when you designed it (this is the default for any Visual Basic form). If the resolution of the system on which your project is running is different from the one on which it was designed, your dialog boxes may appear in unexpected locations.

Dialog boxes are most often centered on-screen. Fortunately, Visual Basic provides an easy tool for centering dialogs—the Screen object.

Certain properties of the display are made available to your programs, namely the `Width` and the `Height`. These properties are accessed using the Screen object as follows:

```
Screen.Width
Screen.Height
```

The position of a form is set using its Left and Top properties to locate the upper-left corner. To display your dialog box in the center of the screen, you must set the `Left` and `Top` properties of the form to a location that puts the center of your dialog box in the center of the screen.

If you drew a line down the center of the screen and put half of your dialog box to the left of that line and half to the right, several things would be true. First, the dialog box would be centered left to right; second, the location of the line would be at `Screen.Width / 2`; and third, the center of your form, from left to right, would correspond to the center of the screen and that location on your form would be `Form.Width / 2`.

The same holds for centering the form from top to bottom. The only difference is that you would substitute the word `Height` for `Width`.

Using this information, you can derive a method to center a form both left to right and top to bottom without regard for the resolution of the display. The code in Listing 8.13 centers any form on any display.

Listing 8.13 Form centering code.

```
Me.Left = Screen.Width / 2 - Me.Width / 2
Me.Top = Screen.Height / 2 - Me.Height / 2
```

Me, in Listing 8.13, refers to the name of the form from which the code is running (the one defining your dialog box). You can copy this code into any form and it will work right away, regardless of the name of the form, because Visual Basic defines Me as the current form.

Displaying Dialog Boxes

Now that you have a custom dialog box, you need to understand the options regarding it being displayed. To display a form, use the Show method. Show loads the form if it has not yet been loaded, and then displays it. If the form is already loaded, Show makes it visible.

The *Show* Method

The format of the Show method is

[*form.*]Show [*style*]

Where *form* is the name of the form you want to show and *style* determines if the form is shown modally or non-modally.

A *style* value of 0 shows a non-modal form. A value of 1 shows a modal form. If *style* is omitted, the form is shown non-modally.

Examples

```
frm.Show
frmInputDialog.Show.1
```

Earlier in this chapter, you learned about modality. The optional style value in the Show method determines whether the form (your dialog box) is shown modally or not. If omitted or set to 0, the form is modeless. If set to 1 the form is shown modally. You will probably want to show your custom dialog boxes *modally* to guarantee that the information is immediately dealt with.

Show's alter ego is Hide. Hide does exactly what its name implies—it hides the form.

The *Hide* Method

The format of the Hide method is

> [*form.*]Hide

Where *form* is the name of the form you want to hide. When hidden, a form is not unloaded. Instead, its Visible property is merely set to False.

Example

> formSubForm5.Hide

Hide does nothing more than set the form's Visible property to False. Show, on the other hand, sometimes does more than set the Visible property to True. If a form is not yet loaded, Show first loads it and then ensures it is visible.

If Show loads a form, then why do you need Load? Load enables you to load a form without showing it. Preloading forms can greatly reduce the delay between showing different forms. If all your forms are loaded when the application starts, then you will be able to switch between them quickly because they are already in memory and Visual Basic doesn't have to retrieve them from disk.

The *Load* and *Unload* Statements

The format of the Load and Unload statements is

> Load *form*
> Unload *form*

Where *form* is the name of the form to be loaded or unloaded.

Examples

> Load frmDialog1
> Unload frmMiscDetail

To load a form without showing it, set its Visible property to False at design time. When it is loaded (via Load), it will be in memory, but not displayed. If loaded with Show, it will be displayed immediately.

From Here...

Dialog boxes are an important part of many Windows applications because they provide a primary means of exchanging information with the user. In this chapter, you learned the following:

- How to use the MsgBox statement to display a dialog box.

- How to specify which icons should appear in a message box.

- How to specify which buttons appear in a message box.

- What the InputBox$ does.

- How to modify the message and default text in an input box.

- How to create a custom dialog box.

- What modality is and how it affects the behavior of your dialog boxes.

Chapter 9
Debugging

Debugging is the process of removing bugs. You wouldn't have to debug your programs if you just didn't put bugs into them in the first place. Unfortunately, programming is a process that is prone to errors. It is sometimes difficult for you to express your ideas with words and after all, words are a significant part of what you use to program computers.

In this chapter, you will learn how you can use the tools provided with Visual Basic to debug your programs. You will also learn some techniques that you can apply during the development process—techniques that will greatly diminish the potential for bugs creeping into your programs in the first place.

What Are Bugs?

If you look good in a programmer's dictionary, you will find that bugs are errors either in hardware or software that cause a computer operation to malfunction. That is not all, however. Bugs also can cause hardware or software to function differently than you would expect. The bottom line is that bugs can cause you hours and hours of headaches when you are programming.

Bugs of many different types can creep into your programming code. These typically fall into only a few categories, however:

- Syntax-related
- Logic-related
- Operation-related

Syntax-Related Errors

Just as grammar is important in ensuring what you say is understood by other people, syntax is vital in making Visual Basic understand what you want done by the computer. Like your ever-watchful mother and father correcting your use of "ain't" and other grammatical mistakes, Visual Basic flags you when it doesn't understand your use of its language. This flagging generally occurs when you attempt to run the program or compile it.

Correct syntax, however, doesn't guarantee a working program. At least not if "working" means that the program performs the intended task. Consider the following, grammatically correct, sentence.

The far off chickens meow as the blinding flash of darkness settles.

What? Chicken meow? Blinding darkness? This is nonsense. Yet, it complies with the grammatical requirements of English. In the same way, you can write syntactically correct programs for Visual Basic that have the same chance of executing properly as the sentence above has of being understood.

Syntax errors are relatively easy to fix, particularly because Visual Basic points out to you where the error occurred and gives you a bit of information to help understand what is happening.

Logic-Related Errors

Logic, in computers, typically means the process and order in which tasks are accomplished. For example, you may want to display information on-screen about the contents of a file. It appears that the records display properly, but for some reason, the subtotals don't come out right. Chances are good that this is a logic error—there is something wrong in the code that is causing the wrong figures to add up.

Logic errors can be the most tedious and troublesome errors to find and correct. This is because you typically have to take a "larger approach" view of your program, trying to figure out what happened where and why.

Operation-Related Errors

Operation-related errors are closely related to logic errors, but there are some subtle differences. Operation errors are the kind that generally result from surpassing the limits of the tools you are using. For example, suppose you have written a program and one of the following occurs:

- You exceed the storage capability of a variable.

- You attempt to do a division, and the divisor is zero.

- You surpass the precision of a data type.

Each of these results in incorrect data being used, and the second one will result in an error when it is encountered. These types of errors can be detected and compensated for, however, if you think through how your program will be used.

Why Are Bugs a Problem?

The manufacturer of a computer goes through several major steps to get the machine into your hands.

1. Design of the computer.

2. Placement of components upon circuit boards.

3. Attachment of circuit boards and other subsystems (power supply, disk drives, and so on) to the chassis and interconnection with other components.

4. Shipment to the vendor.

After the manufacturer completes these steps, you can purchase your computer.

At any step along the way you can be introduced to a defect that will render your new machine inoperable. If your computer isn't designed properly, it will never work. If the parts were plugged into the wrong locations on the circuit board, you'll need a new one. If the power supply wasn't wired to the circuit board properly, you'll probably need a whole new machine.

Suppose a part was misplaced in step 2. If there wasn't any testing along the way, all the other labor and material that goes into the computer is worthless. The machine won't work and the manufacturer will incur significant cost in replacing it.

If the circuit board is tested immediately after part insertion (as they are), however, the mistake would be found and corrected at a time when the cost is minimal.

As a rule, mistakes that go uncorrected cost ten times as much to fix at the next major processing step. If two steps are skipped before the mistake is caught then the cost is 100 times what it would have been had it been corrected immediately. This is why testing occurs at each major step of most manufacturing processes.

The time it takes you to fix a bug in your program works exactly the same way. If you have an error in your basic design you might have to redo the entire application. The time expense in this case is enormous. If you mistype something in a code module and have to track it down after the entire program is complete, it's not as bad as a design flaw. But it can still be time-consuming, especially when you consider that most of these errors are avoidable.

So, before you learn about the techniques for removing bugs, it is only appropriate that you review some steps to help prevent them from occurring in the first place.

Keeping Bugs Out

This book has already introduced you to several good practices for keeping bugs out of your programs. Because they are so important, take a moment to review them and learn about a few new ones.

- *Use meaningful variable names.* When you are concentrating on programming, it is easy to forget what a variable named x or y2 is for. It takes much less effort to recall the purpose of a variable called OuterLoopCounter or MaxCharsPerLine. Every little bit helps and the less you need to concentrate on what a variable is used for, the more you can concentrate on how you are using it.

- *Declare all variables.* Explicit declaration prevents errors due to misspelling. It also guards against another error—data-type confusion. When a variable is undeclared, it most often assumes the type of Variant. Because Variants can hold almost anything, you will not get an error when you assign a string value to a Variant that you intended only to hold numbers or vice versa.

- *Keep procedures short.* Each Function and Sub procedure should perform one specific task—no more and no less. If you fit all the code in a procedure on-screen at once, it is easier to understand. Again, the fewer details, the more you can concentrate on the real task.

- **Test functionality as you go.** Like the manufacturing example given earlier in the chapter, much of your code serves as a basis for later programming stages. By testing each function and subroutine independently, you can isolate errors that, when fixed immediately (while the code is fresh in your mind), aren't terribly expensive to fix. If you don't find the error for a day or more, you may have forgotten how the code functions and will need to spend valuable time recalling its purpose. If the error isn't found until after other code has built upon that procedure, there is the chance that you will not only need to modify the routine in which the error appears, but also those that use it. Catch and fix your mistakes as early as possible.

- **Verify your design before programming.** If your algorithms are faulty to begin with, no amount of programming will fix them. Although you may be eager to implement your ideas and start coding immediately, you must resist the temptation. The number of errors that are tracked to faulty logic is surprising. This type of error is very costly to fix because often most of the program must be rewritten.

- **Add meaningful comments to your procedures.** Even if your program works correctly now, at some time in the future you may want to add features, or someone else may be charged with maintaining it. Code without useful comments is like a jigsaw puzzle—a challenge, at best. Commenting your code is like writing assembly instructions on the pieces of the puzzle—they make life much easier. It is good to comment the purpose of each procedure. Usually a line or two at the beginning describing what values are expected, what the routine does, and what, if any, values are returned.

What is Debugging?

As you learned earlier in the chapter, debugging is the process of removing bugs from your program. How hard it is to get rid of errors will depend on many things: the complexity of your program, the variability of your data, the design process you went through, and your temperament.

Many people say that debugging is actually an art. There is an element of truth in this, because programming is also an art. Some people can sit down in front of a computer, look at code, and immediately comprehend what is wrong. Others can labor for hours, staring at the same code over and over before getting a glimpse of what the problem is.

The programmer, by nature, is also a debugger—you have to be. After all, you understand your programming code more intimately than anyone else. You are not left to fend for yourself, however. Visual Basic provides a series of tools that you can use to debug your programs. The balance of this chapter will help you understand what those tools are and how you can use them in your debugging efforts.

Getting Rid of Bugs

Even if you exercise all the precautions mentioned earlier in this chapter, it always seems that somehow bugs still manage to get through the cracks. This has nothing to do with experience or effort; it simply seems to be a fact of life. Thus, you will need to learn how to use the Visual Basic debugging tools—it is inevitable.

When it comes to debugging, the best teacher is experience; thus, you should "learn by doing." With that in mind, try to design the form shown in figure 9.1. You will need to place two text boxes, one label, and two command buttons.

Fig. 9.1
The form for the
test program.

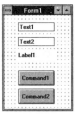

After you create the form, enter the short program shown in Listing 9.1. Don't be alarmed if you see bugs right away—they are supposed to be there. You will learn how to use the tools to uncover and remove these bugs.

Listing 9.1 Bug-ridden program.

```
Sub Command1_Click ()
   Label1 = Text1 + Text2
End Sub

Sub Command2_Click ()
   For LocalCount = 10 To 1
      Label1 = LocalCount
   Next LocalCount
End Sub
```

The Click procedure for Command1 should add the numbers you type in Text1 and Text2, showing the result in Label1. The Click procedure for Command2 is supposed to count down from 10 to 1, displaying the current value in Label1.

Now run your program. So far, so good. Visual Basic didn't inform you of any errors, so things are looking bright. Type a number in Text1 and Text2, and press Command1. What's this? If you look at figure 9.2, you will see that the program gives the wrong result.

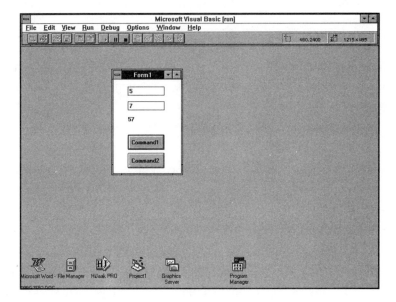

Fig. 9.2
Running the program.

If you add 1 + 1, you get 11; 5 + 7 gives 57. Something is very wrong. There must be a problem with the logic. Try the other command button to see what it does. When you click Command2, you should see the numbers count down from 10 to 1. When you press Command2, however, nothing happens. Are the numbers flashing by so quickly that you can't see them? No, because the last number in the count is 1, and because Label1's caption isn't 1, you know something else is wrong.

You can try to analyze the code you've written to determine what is wrong, but that may not be fruitful since you wrote the code in the first place, and it obviously isn't working. Let's see what Visual Basic has in its bag of debugging tricks to help. After you have a few more tools to work with, you can attack the bugs in this project.

Single Stepping

One of the primary reasons computers are such powerful tools is that they can execute thousands of instructions each second. This ability gives them the blindingly fast speed necessary for calculating hundreds of spreadsheet cells in a second, a task that would take you hours, or perhaps days.

If your program isn't behaving the way you expected, this speed can present a problem. How do you isolate a bug to a particular area of your program if thousands of lines are zinging by every second. There is no way for you to see what is happening.

Single stepping is part of the solution to this problem. As its name implies, single stepping lets you step through your program one line at a time. To single step, select **S**ingle Step from the **D**ebug menu (or press F8). Alternatively, you can click the toolbar button for single stepping; it has a single footprint on its face. The first line of code in your program will be executed and the program will be paused, awaiting your next command.

Pause is a special mode of Visual Basic. When paused, the program is neither terminated nor running. It isn't executing, but it hasn't been unloaded from memory. One of the most advantageous things you can do when a Visual Basic program is paused is examine memory variables.

Figure 9.3 shows your test program in the pause state. It really doesn't look much different from when you really run your program; you should see both your form and the Debug window. In the next section, you will start to learn what you can do with the Debug window, and why it will become your best friend when you are perfecting your programs.

Fig. 9.3
Single stepping through your program.

What's Its Value? When a program is paused (you are single stepping through it), you can examine the value of variables contained in the current procedure. Variables in other procedures are not visible unless they have been declared as Global variables (see Chapter 7).

You should already be single stepping through your program, as described in the previous section. Your program is now waiting for your input. Enter a number in the first text box, and another one in the second text box. So far there is no difference between single stepping and running your program like normal.

Take the next normal step of clicking Command1. Visual Basic now begins to behave differently from normal. Instead of seeing your result right away, a Code window appears and you can see the Click procedure for Command1. The only thing different from a regular Code window is that the first line of the procedure is highlighted, as shown in figure 9.4.

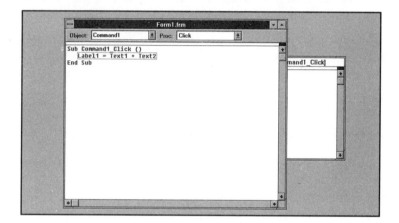

Fig. 9.4
The Click procedure for Command1.

Notice that the Code window overlays the Debug window a bit. You may need to adjust window sizes and position so you can see both windows. You need to do this because you will be using the Debug window shortly.

Remember the problem with Command1? Label1 showed the two numbers concatenated instead of added. Look at the variables and see if you can determine why.

Using your mouse, highlight Text1 in the Command1 procedure code. Now click the Specs (eyeglasses) tool on the toolbar. The Instant Watch window appears, as shown in figure 9.5. This window contains the expression you are evaluating, Text1, and its current value. Nothing seems wrong so far—the value of the variable is set to what you entered. Click the Cancel button to cancel this window. If you use the same process to examine Text2, you'll find that it also contains the correct number.

Fig. 9.5

The Instant Watch window.

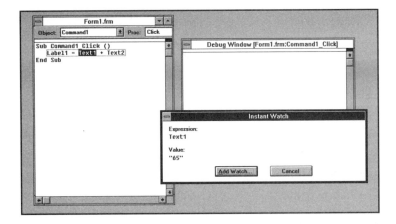

Now evaluate the entire expression by highlighting Text1 + Text2 and clicking the Specs icon. The Instant Watch window shows that the two values are concatenated; they are not added as expected. Apparently there is something wrong with the formula, even though the individual variables in the formula are correct. Ahh! You have narrowed your problem down to a logic error in your formula.

Because there is only one operator in this formula (the plus sign), it is easy to find the problem. The next step is to look in the on-line help to discover how the plus operator is supposed to work. Highlight the plus sign and press F1; this calls up the context-sensitive help. Reading the information displayed on the screen, you can discover that if the operands (Text1 and Text2) are strings, the plus sign concatenates them. The problem your program is exhibiting is that it is interpreting the numbers you have entered as strings and therefore isn't adding them!

To fix this problem and make the plus sign work the way you want it to, you must use numeric values. You do this by converting the operands into numeric values. One way to do this is to use the Val function, which (as you learned earlier in the book) converts strings into numeric values. To make this change, follow these steps:

1. Stop your program, which returns you to Visual Basic's design screen.

2. Double-click the Command1 button. The Code window for the Click procedure appears.

3. Change the instructions so they look like what is shown in Listing 9.2.

4. Close the Code window.

Listing 9.2 The modified procedure.

```
Sub Command1_Click ()
    Label1 = Val(Text1) + Val(Text2)
End Sub
```

Now you can run the program and verify that Command1 works correctly.

Stepping by Procedures. So far you have learned how to single step through your program and examine variables, an immense aid in determining where something has gone wrong. You can figure out (by hand, if necessary) what value a variable should contain at a certain point in the program, and you can compare that with the value it actually contains. If the two are different, you can backtrack and determine where things went wrong.

While you are single stepping through a procedure, you may come across a program line that calls another procedure. If you continue single stepping by clicking the single-step icon (the one with the single footprint on it), you will see the code for that procedure and single step through it as well. If you are confident the error does not lie in the procedure, you may not want to do this. You may want to skip that procedure, instead of executing right through it. Visual Basic allows you to do this by using a *procedure step*.

Procedure steps execute procedures at full speed. They don't skip the procedure; they just run it at its normal speed, which usually results in an immediate return. To step by procedure, use the toolbar icon that contains two footprints. If the next line of code is not a procedure call, the procedure step button will behave as a single step.

Breakpoints

Stepping through your program a line at a time can quickly become tedious—particularly if you have to step through large amounts of code that have already been tested. Even stepping a procedure at a time can be time-consuming in a large program. Isn't there a way to get right to the source of the suspected problem? Yes! This is why Visual Basic allows you to set breakpoints.

A *breakpoint* is a setting you assign to a line of code which pauses the execution of your program when that line is encountered. A breakpoint is different from an End statement. End terminates the execution of your program and removes it from memory. A breakpoint temporarily pauses your program, allowing you to probe memory, and then continue on from the point at which you *broke* execution.

Breakpoints are a convenience; they allow you to execute your program up to a certain point at full speed. You can then examine the value of variables and step a line, or a procedure, at a time to observe your program's behavior.

Setting a Breakpoint. Setting a breakpoint is easy. While your program is stopped or paused, position the cursor on the line at which you want Visual Basic to stop. Now select **T**oggle Breakpoint from the **D**ebug menu (or press F9). That line will appear highlighted, meaning that the breakpoint has been set.

When you later run the program and Visual Basic encounters the line at which you have set a breakpoint, it will do three things:

- Pause the program.

- Display a Code window containing the module with the breakpoint.

- Wait for your command.

At this point, you can apply any other debugging tool you want so you can determine where the error lies.

> ### Note
>
> When Visual Basic pauses due to encountering a breakpoint, it doesn't execute the line at which it stops. That line is the next line that will be executed.

Debugging Using Breakpoints. If you use a breakpoint in conjunction with single stepping, you will see why Command2 isn't working properly. Set a breakpoint on the first executable line in the Command2_Click procedure.

Now run your program and click Command2. Visual Basic shows the procedure containing the breakpoint, as shown in figure 9.6.

Now use the single step tool to start through the procedure. The first thing you notice is that Visual Basic stepped right over the For...Next loop in your code. How could that have happened? If you examine the first line closely, applying the information you learned in Chapter 6, you will see that the

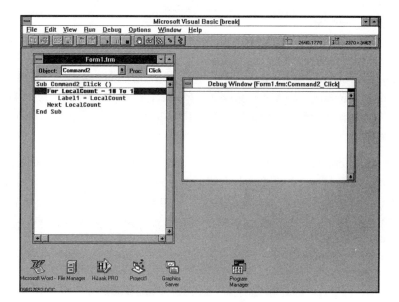

Fig. 9.6

The Click procedure for Command2.

LocalCount loop starts with the value 10, and that the next value in the loop will be 11. What you had intended, however, was for the loop to count backwards, from 10 to 1.

Aha! The problem seems to be that you forgot the Step -1 portion of the For...Next loop, which would have made that happen. Add Step -1 to your code, and it will work as expected. You can single step through to see that each value is displayed, as expected.

The next step is to run the program at full speed to make sure it works properly. Before you can do this, however, you must remove the breakpoint. If you don't, then Visual Basic will dutifully stop each time it comes to the beginning of the Click procedure for Command2.

To remove a breakpoint, stop your program and position the cursor on the line that contains the breakpoint. Then, select **T**oggle Breakpoint from the **D**ebug menu. When you do, the breakpoint (and the telltale highlight) is removed.

After the breakpoints are removed, you can run your program at full speed. You'll only see the last value (1) on-screen, however, because the For...Next loop is executed so quickly.

Tip

It is not unusual during a debugging session to have several different breakpoints set in your program. If you want to remove all the breakpoints in your program at the same time, you can do so by choosing Clear All Breakpoints from the Debug menu.

Watch Expressions

Earlier you learned how you can use the Instant Watch tool (the Specs icon) to examine the contents of a variable or the results of a formula while your program is running. What if you want to watch the value over the course of the entire program, however? Continually selecting the Instant Watch tool could get very tedious. Fortunately, Visual Basic provides the Instant Watch tool to help in this example.

Setting a watch, which in many ways is similar to setting a breakpoint, allows you to monitor the value of any variable in your program. Both the variable name and its value are continually shown in the Debug window. To set a watch expression, select the variable to watch by highlighting it. Then select **A**dd Watch from the **D**ebug menu. You will then see the Add Watch dialog box, shown in figure 9.7.

Fig. 9.7

The Add Watch dialog box.

The Add Watch dialog box allows you to modify exactly what Visual Basic does while it watches the variable. If you only want to continually monitor the value of the variable, you can simply click the OK button. The variable you selected has now been added to the list of watch values. You can add more if you want.

If you run your program, the name of the variable appears in the Debug window, as shown in figure 9.8. Notice that next to the variable name is the phrase <Unable To Evaluate>. Visual Basic can only show you the value of a variable when it is in context. A variable is in context only when you are inside the procedure in which it is declared (although Global variables are always in context).

You can pause Visual Basic while your variable is in context by placing a breakpoint on the last executable line in the procedure in which the variable is declared.

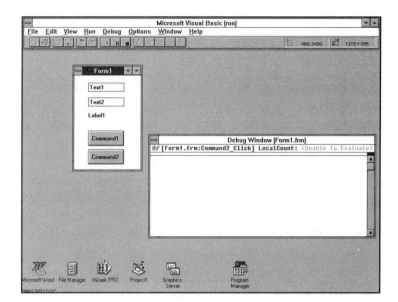

Fig. 9.8
Running a
program with a
watch expression
set.

Breaking on Watches. If you set a breakpoint inside the loop, your program
will break each time the breakpoint is encountered. By using watches, however, you can cause Visual Basic to break the loop only when the loop
counter has reached a particular value. This approach is much more efficient
than debugging. To see how it works, stop your program and follow these
steps:

1. Display the `Click` procedure for `Command2`.

2. Highlight the `LocalCount` variable in the beginning of the `For...Next`
   loop.

3. Choose **A**dd Watch from the **D**ebug menu. The Add Watch dialog box
   appears, as shown earlier in figure 9.8.

4. In the Expression text box, enter a formula that defines when you
   want the program stopped. For example, you can enter the formula
   LocalCount = 4.

5. In the Watch Type box at the bottom of the dialog box, select the Break
   When Expression Is True option.

6. Click OK.

The watch is now added. If you run your program you will find that Visual Basic pauses and enters the Debug mode when the loop is encountered and LocalCount reaches 4.

Editing a Watch. As you are debugging your programs, it is not unusual to set a watch expression and then later need to change it. For example, you may decide that you want your program to break when a particular variable contains the value 125 instead of 80. To edit a watch, just select the **E**dit Watch option from the **D**ebug menu. You will then see a list of watch expressions that have been set in your program, as shown in figure 9.9.

Fig. 9.9
The watch list.

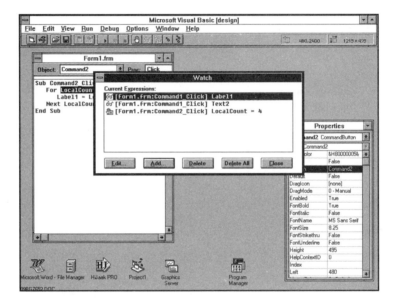

The icons at the left of each watch expression indicate what type of watch has been set. If you see eyeglasses, then Visual Basic only monitors the value. If you see an upraised hand, as shown to the left of the third item in figure 9.9, then Visual Basic will break when the expression is True.

To edit one of the watch expressions, use the mouse to select it from the list of watch expressions. Then click the Edit button. You will see the same dialog box shown earlier in figure 9.8. Using this dialog box, you can change the watch expression and save it again.

Note

Notice on the watch list there are also buttons that allow you to delete watch expressions, either individually or collectively. This is the manner in which Visual Basic allows you to delete watches you previously set.

From Here...

Debugging is typically the final step in program development, but it also can be the most frustrating. Effective debugging takes time, effort, and talent. In this chapter, you learned how you can use Visual Basic tools to debug your programs. In particular, you learned the following:

- The different types of bugs you may encounter.

- Techniques you can use to keep bugs out of your programs in the first place.

- What single stepping is, and how you use it to debug.

- How you can step over entire procedures.

- How to set breakpoints.

- What watches are, and how to set and edit them.

Chapter 10

File Handling

All the Visual Basic programs you have created thus far have accessed information typed in by an end user or hard-coded into your forms and modules. Although this may be sufficient for some programs, you will inevitably need to read data from or write data to a disk file.

Unless you use data files, your programs will never be able to *remember* what the user did the last time he ran the program. Data files are used to store information so the information can be retrieved at some time in the future when you run your Visual Basic program again.

Sometimes files are used to store configuration information such as the user's name and their preferred options. Other times, files are used to *remember* aspects such as the last file that was open and the position of all the windows that were on-screen. Other times, data files are used to store *database information* such as data about customers and orders. All these reasons and many more are valid reasons to use data files in a Visual Basic program.

In this chapter, you will learn the types of data files that you may need to access from within a Visual Basic program, and cover how to do so using the Visual Basic programming language.

File Types

Files are used for a wide variety of purposes on computers. Almost every commercial program uses files in one way or another. These programs create and maintain files with information for their own use or to share with other programs.

There are numerous types of files that you can have on your computer. Typically the file's extension (the last three characters of the filename; the ones after the period) identifies what type of file it is, although nothing forces this identification. You could easily rename .BAS files to have an .EXE extension, but that would not make it run when you click it in the File Manager!

Visual Basic uses quite a few file types: .FRM files for your form's source code, .BAS files for your module's source code, .MAK files for your project files, .VBX files for custom controls, and so on.

Although each file extension typically identifies the type, most file types are only understood by the program that uses them. DOS, which provides all the file support for Windows, does not know one type of file from the next—at least not from the filename alone. Typically, DOS only sees a file as being a series of characters that can be interpreted in any number of ways. The *format* of a file is usually determined by the program that uses it.

For example, DOS does not know or care what a .FRM file is; only Visual Basic knows and cares. This is not true for all file types, of course. Most notably, DOS knows that an .EXE file is an executable file that can be run from Windows and possibly from the DOS command line.

Although DOS does not typically care about specific types of files, there are different formats that can be used by and are used by various programs. You will need to read and update each of these formats differently. The remainder of this section will discuss these different kinds of formats:

- ASCII text files

- Foreign file formats

- Import/Export formats

- Initialization (.INI) files

- Simple multiple record databases

ASCII Text Files

ASCII stands for American Standard Code for Information Interchange, and it defines standard characters for interchanging information on a computer. In ASCII, each character is assigned a numeric code that is used to represent and store that character in a file. The printable characters defined by ASCII are #32 (a space) through #126 (a tilde: "~").

A true *ASCII text file* is a file that contains a series of printable characters separated by a carriage return (ASCII value of 13) and a line-feed character (ASCII value of 10). Each of these carriage return/line-feed pairs denotes the end of a line and the beginning of another line. Figure 10.1 illustrates what a four-line ASCII text file looks like conceptually.

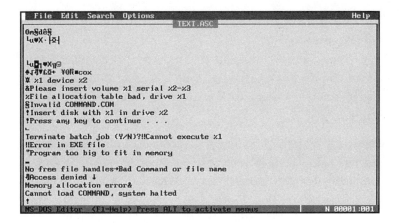

Fig. 10.1
A four-line ASCII text file.

ASCII text files are probably the most common file format used by your PC. Virtually every program that can read and write files can read and write ASCII text files. Both the AUTOEXEC.BAT and CONFIG.SYS on your computer are ASCII text files. The TYPE command in DOS displays an ASCII text file. Windows NotePad allows you to edit and save ASCII text files. Figure 10.2 shows Notepad with CONFIG.SYS loaded.

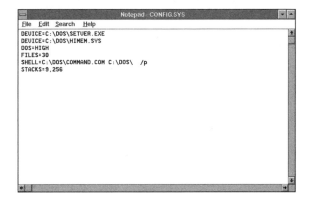

Fig. 10.2
Windows Notepad with CONFIG.SYS loaded.

In addition, Visual Basic project files (those ending in .MAK), form files (those ending in .FRM), and module files (those ending in .BAS) can be stored as ASCII text files. Windows .INI files are ASCII text. Every Windows word processor on the market can import an ASCII text file into their document format, and all of them can create one.

Visual Basic provides statements and functions that make reading and writing ASCII text files line by line a breeze. Those statements will be covered in detail later in this chapter.

Foreign File Formats

Many programs maintain information in their own special file formats. These formats are simply layouts that were created for use with the program because the program's developers decided it was best for them to store their data in that manner.

There are many examples of different types of data formats. For example, database programs like dBASE and FoxPro store their data in .DBF files. Lotus 1-2-3 originally stored its spreadsheets in .WKS files. Word for Windows stores its documents in .DOC files and its templates in .DOT files. Ami Pro stores its documents in .SAM files. And the list goes on and on.

Each of these file formats was originally designed by the developer(s) of the program. Some of these formats have been published so that anyone who wants to read and update them can do so. Other formats are considered trade secrets and the only way to figure them out (short of hiring a spy) is to spend a lot of time with a program that lets you look at each character in the file—although this is much like trying to learn French by picking up a book written in French and simply trying to read it. Some people can do it, but it will probably take a long time and a lot of perseverance!

Provided you know the format of a specific file, you can write routines in Visual Basic to read, write, and update any foreign file type you want. This writing is done using the *binary file* processing capability of Visual Basic, which is covered later in this chapter.

Import/Export Formats

Although many programs maintain information in files of their own format, there are several common file interchange formats used for importing and exporting into and out of programs. These common formats are understood by many programs and facilitate the transfer of information from one program to the next.

Examples of these format types are the Rich Text Format (.RTF) for transferring word processing files from one word processor to the next. Another example is an older format known as the Data Interchange Format (.DIF) which is used to transfer information from one spreadsheet program to another. There are many other special formats in use today, and there will be many more designed and used in the future.

Often these import/export file formats are simply specially formatted ASCII text files. These types of files can be easily viewed and edited with a text editor such as Notepad. Even so, these files contain additional information needed by programs during the import of the data.

Visual Basic provides direct support for an import/export format often referred to as a *delimited text file* or a *quotes-and-commas* format because each character field in the file is quoted, and all fields are delimited with commas. Listing 10.1 provides a sample of a quotes-and-commas format file.

Listing 10.1 Sample delimited text file.

```
"Mike Schinkel",31,"Atlanta","GA"
"Michelle Brookshire",26,"Clermont","GA"
"Matt Adams",30,"Buford","GA"
"Traci Detchon",36,"Smyrna","GA"
```

Using either Visual Basic's ASCII or binary file processing capability, you have the tools you need to process any type of import/export file that you will find.

Initialization (.INI) Files

Another use of ASCII text files is the special .INI format used by Windows and so many of its programs. These programs create and maintain their own .INI files, and most likely your Visual Basic programs should too.

Windows uses WIN.INI and SYSTEM.INI, which are configuration files that specify Windows current configuration. Figure 10.3 shows SYSTEM.INI and WIN.INI loaded in SysEdit, a program found in the \WINDOWS\SYSTEM directory that allows an experienced Windows user to modify his or her configuration files.

Although you could write routines to read and update .INI files using Visual Basic's ability to process ASCII files, Windows provides specific functions (known as *API functions*) that VB can call to manipulate .INI files.

Fig. 10.3
SysEdit showing
WIN.INI and
SYSTEM.INI.

File Basics

Because data files are external to your programs, you must take certain steps to allow your program to access the information contained in the files. Essentially, your Visual Basic program must establish a line of communication with a file before it can process it. When you finish using a file, you should cut off that line of communication because each open line of communication requires resources to maintain.

Opening a File

In the same way you open the door of a filing cabinet before you can browse through its files, your Visual Basic program must open a file before it can read or update its contents. The statement to do this is Open. Using only its most basic options, you can open files for reading (Input), writing (Output), or appending (Append).

Opening Data Files
The basic format for the Open statement is

    Open *filename$* [for *mode*] As [#]*filenum*

You must use Open before attempting to read or write from the file.
filename$ must be a valid DOS filename. *mode* can be any of Input,
Output, or Append. *filenum* can be any integer from 1 to 255.

Examples

    Open "C:\AUTOEXEC.BAT" For Input As #1
    Open "ERRORLOG.TXT" For Append As 2

When you open a file, you must specify a *file number*. This file number is used to refer to the line of communication between your program and the file on disk. Whenever you need to read from, write to, or otherwise manipulate an open file, you will need to use the file number you specified when you opened the file.

Note

Although it is okay in small programs to specify a literal number when you open a file, such as 1, 2, or 7, it is much better to use the FreeFile function in larger programs to grab the lowest unused file number for use with your Open statement. To use FreeFile, store the number it returns into a variable and then use that variable whenever you need to refer to the file in the Open statement or any other statement or function that expects a file number as a parameter. For example:

```
Dim FileNum
FileNum = FreeFile()
Open "C:\AUTOEXEC.BAT" For Input As FileNum
```

The mode that you specify when you open the file is important as well. If you open a file for Input, then you will only be able to read from the file. If you open it for Output, you will only be able to write to the file, and Visual Basic will start writing to the file at the beginning. If you instead specify Append, you will only be able to write to the file, but Visual Basic will start writing to the file at the end if the file already exists on disk. You will learn how to both read *and* write to the same open file later in this chapter.

Caution

If you open a file for Output and that file already exists, all the data previously in the file will be erased. Be very careful with this and only open a file for Output when you know it does not exist, or if you definitely want to start over with it from scratch. Use the following function to determine if a file exists:

```
Function FileExists(FName As String) As Integer
    If Dir$(FName,0) = "" Then
        FileExists = False
    Else
        FileExists = True
    End If
End Function
```

Handling File Errors

When you open a file, there is unfortunately a good chance that something could go wrong—for example, the file could be missing. Because of this fact, you must be sure to provide error handling for any routines that open files.

The easiest way for you to handle an error on the Open statement is to use On Error Resume Next and then check the Err function afterwards. The Err function will return a nonzero number identifying the error if an error did occur on the Open statement. The values returned by the Err function are listed under "Trapable Errors" in Visual Basic's Help system.

Listing 10.2 illustrates how to trap and identify file errors; you yourself will have to determine what to do in case of an error, as the error handling required for each is likely to be different.

Listing 10.2 Handling file errors.

```
Dim FileNum As Integer
FileNum = FreeFile
On Error Resume Next
Open "C:\AUTOEXEC.BAT" For Input As FileNum
If Err <> 0 Then
    MsgBox ("File Error: " + Str$(Err))
End If
```

Reading Data Files

After you have opened a file, the easiest way to read from it is to read the entire file. You can do this using a combination of the two functions Input$ and Lof. The Input$ function reads data from a file and returns it as a string.

Reading Data from Files

Use the Input$ function with a file opened using the Input mode of the Open statement. The basic format for the Input$ function is

> data$ = Input$(*bytes*, [#]*filenum*)

Where *bytes* is the number of bytes to read from the file into data$, and *filenum* specifies which file to read. This *filenum* should be the same number used on the As clause of the Open statement.

Example

```
Open "C:\CONFIG.SYS" For Input As #1
text = Input$(1024, #1)
```

The Lof function returns the total number of characters contained in an open file (that is, its size in bytes).

Obtaining the Length of a Data File

The Lof function returns the number of bytes in a file (its length). The basic format for the Lof function is

```
length = Lof(filenum)
```

Where *filenum* specifies which file to read and should be the same number used on the As clause of the Open statement.

Example

```
FileSize = Lof(1)
```

You can use the Input$ function with the Lof function to retrieve an entire file into a string variable. This technique is one of the simplest ways of reading a file and care should be taken not to read a very large file in this manner. Listing 10.3 shows how to read an entire file into a variable using Input$ and Lof (note that it ignores error handling for the sake of brevity).

Listing 10.3 Reading files with *Input$* and *Lof*.

```
Dim FileNum As Integer
Dim Text As String
FileNum = FreeFile
Open "C:\AUTOEXEC.BAT" For Input As FileNum
Text= Input$(Lof(FileNum), FileNum)
```

> **Caution**
>
> Although it is difficult to say exactly how large a file you can read in this manner, a good rule for a maximum may be 32K, or 32,768 bytes. This is half the maximum string size and is likely to work without a problem. You could load files larger than this, but it would be unreliable. Processing the file in smaller segments would be a better solution, as you will see later in this chapter.

Closing Files

Just as it is a good idea to close your file cabinet drawers after you are through with them (so you don't bang your shin!), you should also close your program's data files as soon as you no longer need to have them open. A simple

Close statement is all that is required to release the line of communication between the program and the file.

Tip

It is a good idea for you to close a file as soon as possible to avoid corruption. Because Visual Basic does not always write information to the disk when you ask it to (it waits until an internal output buffer is full), you cannot be sure that what you sent to the file is *actually* written to the file until you close it. If users get in the habit of turning off their computers before exiting your program, or if they have frequent power outages, any open files may become corrupt. Because it is better to be safe than sorry, close the file as soon as you can.

Closing a Data File

The Close statement releases the file opened with the Open statement and forces all data written to that file to disk. The basic format for the Close statement is

```
Close [[#]filenum]
```

Where *filenum* specifies which file to close and should be the same number used on the As clause of the Open statement. If *filenum* is omitted, then all the open files are closed.

Examples

```
Close #1
Close 2
```

Loading a File

In the interest of providing a complete example, Listing 10.4 contains the function LoadFile which, when passed a filename and a numeric variable for an error code, will open a file, read it completely into a string variable, close the file, and then return the file contents. The sample Sub Main in Listing 10.4 illustrates how to call the LoadFile function:

Listing 10.4 Loading a file with *LoadFile*.

```
Sub Main
    Dim iErr As Integer
    Dim Text As String
    Text= LoadFile("C:\AUTOEXEC.BAT",iErr)
    If iErr <> 0 Then
        MsgBox("Error Reading C:\AUTOEXEC.BAT")
    End If
End Sub

Function LoadFile(FName As String, iErr As Integer)
    Dim FileNum As Integer
    FileNum = FreeFile()
    On Error Resume Next
    Open FName For Input As #FileNum
    IErr = Err
    If IErr <> 0 Then
        LoadFile = ""
    Else
        LoadFile = Input$(LOF(FileNum), #FileNum)
        Close (FileNum)
    End If
End Function
```

Types of File Access

There are three modes for Visual Basic programmers to access disk files:

- Sequential-access

- Random-access

- Binary-access

As discussed earlier, each of these three methods of accessing files has its own particular purpose.

Sequential Files

A *sequential file* is one written and read from the beginning to the end, in order, much like how tape is played in a tape player. The typical tape player cannot skip to the next song on the tape; instead, it must play or fast-forward through the entire song.

So, a sequential file is one that you can only read in the order that it was written. The reason for this is there is no predetermined structure, and there are no clues for what data is located where.

Reading ASCII Text Files. A perfect example of a sequential file is an ASCII text file. A text editor such as Notepad reads an ASCII text file line by line into memory, and then later writes the entire file back out to disk, typically overwriting the previous copy of the file.

In your Visual Basic programs, you may want to read ASCII text files so you can modify them. For example, you may want to update your AUTOEXEC.BAT PATH statement. Or, you may want to write a utility to extract information like the names of subroutines and functions from your Visual Basic .FRM and .BAS files. Or, you can choose from a multitude of other tasks you can accomplish.

To read the data in an ASCII text file, you must first open the file for input and then you can use the Line Input# statement.

As mentioned earlier, you can use the Line Input# statement to read a line in an ASCII text file, but ASCII text files often contain more than one line. Obviously, you may need to read more than one line so what do you do? Do you use two Line Input# statements to read two lines, three statements to read three lines, and so on? Of course not! You read lines inside a loop such as a While...Wend loop.

Reading a Line from a File

The basic format for the `Line Input#` statement is

```
Line Input #filenum, line$
```

The `Line Input#` statement reads a line from the file identified by *filenum* into the *line$* string variable.

Examples

```
Dim TextLine As String
Line Input #1, TextLine
```

But that creates another problem. How do you know when you've reached the last line in the file? Easy. Visual Basic provides an `Eof` (end-of-file) function that tells you when you have read the last line in the file (but not before).

As an example, assume you want to write a program that would display all the `Sub` and `Function` declarations in an .FRM file (assuming you save your .FRM's in ASCII).

To write this program, you would need a function that would open the .FRM file, read the file line by line to determine which lines had a `Sub` or `Function` declaration in them, and then return only those lines separated with carriage return-line feeds. `LoadSubDecl`, shown in Listing 10.5, performs exactly this task. The CR/LFs make it possible for you to display the string returned by `LoadSubDecl` using a multiline text box.

Listing 10.5 Loading subroutine and function declarations from an .FRM file.

```
Function LoadSubDecl (FName As String, ErrNum As Integer)
    Dim FileNum As Integer
    Dim TextLine, TempLine As String
    Dim OutLine As String
    Dim CRLF As String
    CRLF = Chr(13) + Chr(10)
    FileNum = FreeFile
    On Error Resume Next
    Open FName For Input As FileNum
    ErrNum = Err
    If ErrNum = 0 Then
        OutLine = ""
        Do Until EOF(FileNum)
```

```
            Line Input #FileNum, TextLine
            TempLine = Left(UCase$(TextLine), 4)
            If TempLine = "SUB " Then
                OutLine = OutLine + TextLine + CRLF
            ElseIf TempLine = "FUNC" Then
                OutLine = OutLine + TextLine + CRLF
            End If
        Loop
        Close FileNum
    End If
    LoadSubDecl = OutLine
End Function
```

Writing to ASCII Text Files. Now that you have read ASCII text files in, you may want to learn how to write them out as well. You write ASCII text files out by using the Print# statement.

Writing a Line to a File

The basic format for the Print# statement is

```
        Print #filenum, line$
```

The Print# statement as shown writes the information contained in the line$ string variable to the file identified by filenum.

Examples

```
        Dim TextLine As String
        TextLine= "Hello World!"
        Print #1, TextLine
```

When you use the Print# statement, it writes your string to the file followed by a CR/LF.

> **Note**
>
> If you want to write to a file but you don't want Print# to write the CR/LF charac-
> ters that define an ASCII file, or if you want to write several values before Print#
> outputs another CR/LF, you can force the Print# statement to omit the CR/LF by
> placing a semicolon after the string. For example:
>
> ```
>     Print #1, "This ";
>     Print #1, "creates ";
>     Print #1, "one ";
>     Print #1, "line."        ' Note no semi-colon here
>
>     Print #1, "This " ; "also " ; "creates " ; "one " ; "line."
> ```

Suppose you want to write a routine that updates the PATH setting in AUTOEXEC.BAT. Writing this routine can be useful if your application consists of multiple .EXE files and you want it to be able to find the .EXEs no matter what the current directory.

To write such a routine, you would need a function that would open up both AUTOEXEC.BAT for input and another temporary file for output. The function FixAutoExec, shown in Listing 10.6, creates a file called AUTOEXEC.NEW with the updated file information.

Listing 10.6 Fixing the *PATH* statement in AUTOEXEC.BAT.

```
Sub Main()
    Dim Fixed As Integer
    Dim iErr As Integer
    Fixed= FixAutoExec("C","C:\MYAPP",iErr)
    If Fixed Then
        MsgBox("AUTOEXEC.NEW Created!")
    Else
        MsgBox("Error creating AUTOEXEC.NEW")
    End If
End Sub

Function FixAutoExec (Drive As String,
                      ➥NewDir As String,
                      ➥ErrNum As Integer) As Integer
    Dim InpFile As Integer
    Dim OutFile As Integer
    Dim TxtLn As String
    Dim Fixed As Integer
    Dim Temp As String
    Dim FileCnt As Integer
    Fixed = False
    On Error Resume Next
    InpFile = FreeFile
    Open Drive + ":\AUTOEXEC.BAT"
    ➥For Input As InpFile
    ErrNum = Err
    If ErrNum = 0 Then
        OutFile = FreeFile
        Open Drive + ":\AUTOEXEC.NEW"
        ➥For Output As OutFile
        ErrNum = Err
        If ErrNum = 0 Then
            Do Until EOF(InpFile)
                Line Input #InpFile, TxtLn
                Temp = Left(UCase$(TxtLn), 5)
                If Temp = "PATH=" Then
                    TxtLn = "PATH=" + NewDir + ";" + Mid$(TxtLn,6)
                End If
                Print #OutFile, TxtLn
```

```
          Loop
            Close OutFile
        End If
        Close InpFile
        Fixed = True
      End If
    FixAutoExec = Fixed
  End Function
```

Of course, the function `FixAutoExec` does not actually update
AUTOEXEC.BAT, it simply creates a new file called AUTOEXEC.NEW with
the updated PATH statement. If you want `FixAutoExec` to actually update
AUTOEXEC.BAT, you will need two statements that have not been covered
yet; `FileCopy` and `Kill`.

Copy a File

The basic format for the `FileCopy` statement is

```
    FileCopy SourceFile$, DestinationFile$
```

The `FileCopy` statement copies the file you specify for *SourceFile*$ to
the filename you specify for *DestinationFile*$.

Example

```
    FileCopy "AUTOEXEC.NEW", "AUTOEXEC.BAT"
```

Delete a File

The basic format for the `Kill` statement is

```
    Kill File$
```

The `Kill` statement deletes the file you specify from the disk.

Example

```
    Kill "AUTOEXEC.NEW"
```

Now that the `FileCopy` and `Kill` statements have been discussed, you can add
the source code in Listing 10.7 to the `FixAutoExec` function in place of the

line that contained "Fixed = True." This line was located near the bottom of the FixAutoExec function. Be sure that you indent your code neatly.

Listing 10.7 Updating AUTOEXEC.BAT with AUTOEXEC.NEW.

```
FileCopy "C:\AUTOEXEC.BAT", "C:\AUTOEXEC.OLD"
If Err = 0 Then
    FileCopy "C:\AUTOEXEC.NEW", "C:\AUTOEXEC.BAT"
End If
If Err = 0 Then
    Kill "C:\AUTOEXEC.NEW"
    Fixed = True
End If
```

Reading Delimited Text Files. As stated earlier, a delimited text file is an ASCII file, but it is an ASCII file for which Visual Basic provides some special processing capabilities. Often you may use these file formats to import from or export to database or spreadsheet programs.

To read delimited text files, you can use the Input# statement whose format is shown in the Syntax at a Glance boxes:

Reading a Line from a Delimited Text File
The basic format for the Input# statement is

Input #*filenum*, *var1* [, *var2*] [..., *varN*]

The Input# statement reads a line from the file identified by *filenum* and parses the information in the file into the variables *var1* through *varN* that you specify.

Example

```
Dim FullName As String * 25
Dim Age As Integer
Dim City As String * 15
Dim State As String * 2
Input #1, FullName, Age, City, State
```

When you use the Input# statement, you must be sure that the file you are reading and the variables you are using coincide in number and in type. If you do not specify enough variables to hold all the data to be read in, or if you specify too few, Visual Basic will get confused and you will end up getting garbage in your variables.

Writing Delimited Text Files. The converse of the Input# statement is the Write# statement. The Write# statement will create a file that can be read back into numerous other programs, or into Visual Basic using the `Input#` statement.

Write a Line to a Delimited Text File

The basic format for the `Write#` statement is

```
Write #filenum, value1 [, value2] [..., valueN]
```

The `Write#` statement writes a delimited text file line using the values *value1* through *valueN* to a file identified by *filenum*.

Example

```
Write #1, "John Deere", 95, "Des Moines","Iowa"
```

Random-Access Files

As compared to a sequential file, a *random-access file* is one that can be read and written in any order. You may want to think of a random-access file as being like a compact disc instead of a cassette tape. Just like a compact disc where you can select and play specific songs (or tracks) in any order, you can read, write, and even update portions of a random-access file in any order.

Random-access files were originally provided to allow the BASIC programmers an easy way to create *databases*. What is a database? A database is simply a collection of related information organized in a structured way. In earlier days, BASIC programmers created relatively sophisticated database applications using random-access files as the tables in a relational database. Today, however, you would probably not want to use random-access files to implement a complex database program. Visual Basic provides much greater database capabilities via the powerful Access Database Engine and through ODBC. (Both of these topics are beyond the scope of this book. For more information, refer to Que's *Using Visual Basic 3*.)

Random-access files are useful if you need to create a relatively simple database or if you need to read and update data that was created or is maintained by an older BASIC application.

Random-Access vs. Sequential Files. Assuming you have decided that using a random-access file is the best solution for your needs, be aware that random-access files provide both benefits and drawbacks when compared to sequential files. Table 10.1 discusses the pros and cons of random-access files.

Table 10.1 Pros and Cons of Random-Access Files	
PROS	**CONS**
Information can be accessed much quicker using random-access files because your program can request to read a specific record only instead of being required to read the entire file.	You will not be able to read random-access files by other programs unless they have been specifically written to recognize your record structures.
You can update the records of a random-access file without having to create a new file.	Records must be fixed-length and thus take up more space than the same information stored in a sequential file.
You can read and write records in a random-access file in any order.	Every record in a random-access file must be exactly the same structure.

Record Variables: User-Defined Types. Processing random-access files means processing records. As such, you must define the records in your file, which is done by using the Type...End Type block statement. After you have defined your structure with Type...End Type, you can create variables using that definition and then store the values contained in these variables directly into the records of your random-access file.

You must be aware of the size of the structure (in bytes) that you create using the Type...End Type statement. This awareness will be important when you open the random file so you can determine how much disk space will be required by your random-access file.

The size in bytes of a record is determined by the sum of the sizes in bytes for each member of your structure. String variables are easy: each character in a string takes one byte, so a string defined as String * 25 occupies 25 bytes in your structure. The number of bytes required by each of the numeric types is a little more difficult to determine. You may want to refer to the information in Chapter 4 where data types are discussed more fully.

As an example, assume you want to add a file of user information to your Visual Basic program. This use would be well-suited for a random-access file because you would likely have no need to read this information with another program; on the contrary, you would probably want this information to be somewhat secure.

Define Record Structures for Random-Access Files

This format for the Type...End Type statement is

```
Type rec_struct
    field1 AS type1
    field2 AS type2
    ...
    fieldN AS typeN
End Type
...
Dim var As rec_struct
```

Use the Type...End Type statement to define the structure of your records for random-access files. rec_struct becomes the name of the new data type, field1 through fieldN are the names of the fields in the structure, and type1 through typeN are their corresponding data types.

The structure name rec_struct then becomes a valid data type and can be used to declare var variables on the Dim statement.

Example

```
Type GolfCart
    Model String * 10
    Color String * 15
    Seats Integer
    Horses Single
End Type

Dim MyCart As GolfCart
MyCart.Model = "Bogie XL"
MyCart.Color = "Fairway Green"
MyCart.Seats = 2
MyCart.Horses = 10
```

Your user information file would likely include the user's full name, user id, user level, password, and birthday so that you can wish him a happy birthday on the appropriate day. In addition, you may want to keep some statistics such as the date of his first use of the system, and the total time that he has spent using the system. The latter necessitates that you maintain the time and date which he started running the program last. Finally, you may want to maintain a field to indicate which records are deleted. Listing 10.8

provides a structure definition for UserStruct that provides this type of information and a declaration for the variable User which is of type UserStruct. Note that you will need to declare your structures in one of your modules (.BAS files), not in your forms (.FRM files).

Listing 10.8 Structure of user info record.

```
Type UserStruct
    UserId As String * 10       'User's ID
    FullName As String * 25     'User's Full Name
    Password As String * 10     'User's Password
    Birthday As String * 10     'User's BirthDay
    UserLevel As String * 1     'User Level 0..3
    FirstUse As String * 10     'Date of first use
    StartTime As Long           'Seconds this run
    StartDate As String * 10    'Date of this run
    TotalTime As Double         'Cum time since start
    UseCount As Integer         'Times in the system
    Deleted As String * 1       'Delete Flag: *
End Type
Dim User As UserStruct
```

The size of the User variable of type UserStruct is 91 bytes: 10 + 25 + 10 + 10 + 1 + 10 + 4 + 10 + 8 + 2 + 1.

Opening Random-Access Files. To open a file for random-access, you should specify For Random on the Open statement instead of Input, Output, Append. In addition, you should specify the record size in bytes using the Len= clause.

Opening Data Files for Random Access.
This format for the Open statement is

Open *filename*$ For Random As [#]*filenum* Len=*reclen*

You must use Open before attempting to read or write from the file. *filename*$ must be a valid DOS filename. *filenum* can be any integer from 1 to 255. *reclen* should be the size of the file's records.

Example

Open "USERS.DAT" For Random As #1 Len=55

> **Note**
>
> When you open a random-access file, you specify the record length using the Len= clause. Although you can hard-code the length, it is more maintainable to let Visual Basic calculate the length itself. By passing the record variable to the Len function (discussed in Chapter 5), you can determine the size in bytes of the record. If you change the record structure as your program evolves, you will not need to modify the Len= clause of the Open statement. For example:
>
> ```
> Dim User As UserStruct
> Open "USERS.DAT" For Random As #1 Len=Len(User)
> ```

Reading Records from Random-Access Files. When you have a file open for random access, you can read any record simply by using the Get statement.

Reading Records from Random-Access Files

This format for the Get statement is

```
Get #filenum, [recnum], recvar
```

The Get statement reads the record identified by *recnum* into the *recvar* variable from the file identified by *filenum*. *recnum* is optional and if omitted, the Get statement will read the next record in the file.

Examples

```
Get #1, 5, User      'Get 5th user record
Get #1, , User       'Get next user record
```

You can omit the record number in the Get statement if you want. Listing 10.9 provides a simple example of reading records from a file sequentially using the Get statement.

Listing 10.9 Example of using the *Get#* statement.

```
'From MODULE1.BAS
Type NameStruct
   First As String * 10
   MI As String * 1
   Last As String * 15
End Type

'From FORM1.FRM
Dim RecCount As Long
Dim i As Integer
```

(continues)

Listing 10.9 Continued

```
Open "names.dat" For Random As #1 Len = 26
RecCount = LOF(1) / 50
ReDim Names(RecCount) As NameStruct
For i = 1 To RecCount
   Get #1, , Names(i)  'No need for recnum
Next I
Close #1
```

Although you have seen how to read records sequentially using the Get statement, you can read them in any order. You only need be careful that you do not read a record that does not yet exist in the file; if you attempt to do so, Visual Basic will trigger an error.

Writing Records to Random-Access Files. Conversely to the Get statement, the Put statement is used to write records to a random-access file.

Writing Records to a Random-Access File
This format for the Put statement is

```
    Put #filenum, [recnum], recvar
```

The Put statement writes the record contained in the *recvar* variable to the record identified by *recnum* in the file identified by *filenum*. *recnum* is optional, and if omitted, the Put statement will write to the *next* record in the file.

Examples

```
    Put #1, 5, User      'Put user var into 5th record
    Put #1, , User       'Put user var into next record
```

Just like the Get statement, you can omit the record number when you call the Put statement.

As an example, assume that you had a form with three text controls for entering first name, middle initial, and last name. Listing 10.10 shows how to write that information to the *current* record (stored in the global variable RecNo) of a random-access file.

Listing 10.10 Example of using the *Get#* statement.

```
'From MODULE1.BAS
Type NameStruct
   First As String * 10
   MI As String * 1
   Last As String * 15
```

```
End Type
Global RecNo As Long

'From FORM1.FRM
Dim FullName As NameStruct
Open "names.dat" For Random As #1 Len = 26
FullName.First = txtFirst.Text
FullName.MI = txtMI.Text
FullName.Last = txtLast.Text
Put #1, RecNo, FullName
Close #1
```

Binary Files

As compared to both sequential and random-access files which access files essentially at the record level, *binary files* are accessed byte by byte. As such, binary files have no limitations whatsoever; you can process a binary file any way you like (assuming that you designed the format of the file). On the other hand, nothing is done for you automatically with binary files; you must determine exactly where to place data into the file and then specify that information to Visual Basic.

> **Note**
>
> Actually, there is no such thing as a *binary* file; any file can be opened for binary access. You will be able to read, write, and update information for every type of file ever created on a personal computer using binary mode, assuming that you know the file's format!

Opening Files for Binary Access. To open a file for binary access, you should specify For Binary on the Open statement. Because binary files are accessed byte by byte, you do not need to specify a Len= clause as you did for random-access files.

Opening Data Files for Binary Access

This format for the Open statement is

```
Open filename$ For Binary As [#]filenum
```

You must use Open before attempting to read from or write to the file. *filename$* must be a valid DOS filename. *filenum* can be any integer from 1 to 255.

Example

```
Open "CUSTOMER.DBF" For Binary As #1
```

Reading from Binary Access Files. When you have opened a file for binary access, you can use the Get statement to read information from the file into variables.

Reading Records from Binary Files

This format for the Get statement is

```
Get #filenum, [bytepos], var
```

The Get statement reads data from the file identified by *filenum*, starting at the position *bytepos*, into the *var* variable. The size of *var* (in bytes) determines how many bytes will be read from the file. *bytepos* is optional and if omitted, the Get statement will read from the file starting at the next byte in the file.

Examples

```
Get #1, 33, FldInfo      'Get to FldInfo from byte 33
Get #1, , FldInfo        'Get to FldInfo from current
```

Writing to Binary-Access Files. Writing to a binary file is as easy as reading; you simply use the Put statement to write information from a variable into the file.

Writing Records to Binary Files

This format for the Put statement is

```
Put #filenum, [bytepos], var
```

The Put statement writes the contents of *var* to the file identified by *filenum*, starting at the position *bytepos*. The size of *var* (in bytes) determines how many bytes will be written to the file. *bytepos* is optional and if omitted, the Put statement will write to the file starting at the next byte in the file.

Examples

```
Put #1, 50, FldInfo      'Put to file starting at byte
                         ➥50
Put #1, , FldInfo        'Put to file immediately
```

Updating the Current Position in a Binary File. If you use binary-access files, you may need to move to a specific position in a file so you can begin accessing a portion of the file in a sequential manner. You can use the Seek statement to update the current file position.

Updating the Current Position in a Binary File
The format for the Seek statement is

```
Seek #filenum, bytepos
```

The Seek statement updates the current file pointer position (for *filenum*) so that the next byte, read or written, is the byte you specified with *bytepos*.

Examples

```
Seek #1, 50     'Move current position to byte 50
```

When you use the Get or Put statements and specify a byte position to start at, it is much like calling the Seek statement and then calling the Get or Put statements without a starting byte position. In other words, the source code in the following two lines of code:

```
Seek #1, 33
Get #1, , FldInfo
```

is identical in effect to this line of code:

```
Get #1, 33, FldInfo
```

You may use the Seek statement just prior to entering a loop. Listing 10.11 shows how to use the Seek statement in this manner for bypassing the file header on a dBASE .DBF file prior to scanning for the first deleted record in the file (one whose record data begins with an asterisk).

Listing 10.11 Using *Seek* with binary-access files.

```
Dim RecData As String
RecData= String$(63)    'Set buffer to 63 bytes
Open "customer.dbf" For Binary As #1
Seek #1, 161            'Move to byte 161
Do
    Get #1, , RecData
Loop Until Eof(1) Or Left$(RecData,1)="*"
Close #1
```

Determining the Current Position in a Binary File. You also can determine the byte position that was last processed and the next byte to process using the two functions Loc and Seek, respectively. By using either of these you can save and later restore your position in a file.

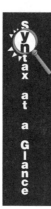

Retrieve the Last Byte Position Processed in a Binary File

The format for the Loc function is

        bytepos = Loc(filenum)

The Loc function returns (into *bytepos*) the last byte position, read or written, in the file identified by *filenum*.

Examples

```
Put #2, 161, "*"    'Write asterisk at pos 161
MsgBox(Loc(2))      'Displays 161
```

Retrieve the Next Byte Position to Process in a Binary File

The format for the Seek function is

        bytepos = Seek(filenum)

The Seek function returns (into *bytepos*) the next byte position, read or written, in the file identified by *filenum*.

Examples

```
Put #2, 161, "*"    'Write 6p6
splays 162
```

You can use Seek (or Loc) to save and later restore your positions in a binary file as shown in Listing 10.12.

Listing 10.12 Saving and Restoring Byte Positions.

```
Dim SavePos As Integer
Open "orders.dbf" For Binary As #3
SavePos = Seek(3)
...                     'Do something here
Seek #3, SavePos        'Return to previous position
```

The Wide Variety of Uses for Binary Files. You have now seen the statements used to access a file on the byte-by-byte level. You can use binary access to allow you to open and read files created by any application, assuming you know the format.

In addition, you can define your own file formats and then write Visual Basic routines to create and then load the information stored in these files.

Binary-access files provide more low-level power than any of the other types of access, and you will likely find yourself using this type of access when the type of information you need to store becomes more and more complex.

Updating .INI Files

Windows and most Windows applications make use of a special type of ASCII file with an extension of .INI (pronounced *Innie*). These .INI files are used to store information about program configuration, and to save information about the state of an application between successive runs of the program.

Windows uses two special files called SYSTEM.INI and WIN.INI in which it stores Windows system-level configuration information and user-level configuration information, respectively. Listing 10.13 shows a portion of SYSTEM.INI so that you can see the format of this file.

Listing 10.13 A portion of SYSTEM.INI.

```
[boot]
386grabber=mach32.3gr
oemfonts.fon=vgaoem.fon
286grabber=vgacolor.2gr
fixedfon.fon=VGAFIX.FON
fonts.fon=VGASYS.FON
display.drv=aw5xga.drv
shell=C:\APPS\DASH\dash.exe
mouse.drv=aw5mouse.drv
network.drv=NETWARE.DRV
language.dll=
comm.drv=comm.drv
keyboard.drv=aw5kbd.drv
system.drv=system.drv
drivers=mmsystem.dll winmm16.dll
SCRNSAVE.EXE=C:\WINDOWS\SSSTARS.SCR
oemfonts=VGAOEM.FON

[keyboard]
subtype=
type=4
keyboard.dll=
oemansi.bin=

[boot.description]
aspect=100,96,96
display.drv=mach32 Driver
displayinf=OEM68800.INF

...much more stuff
```

As you may have noticed, .INI files have various sections that begin with their section name enclosed in square brackets, followed by lines that set identifiers to values using an equal (=) sign.

Although you can process .INI files using the sequential file I/O, the Windows API provides a much better alternative. There are four functions in the Windows API that read and write .INI files; two of them work specifically with WIN.INI and the other two will support any .INI file.

> **Note**
>
> The Windows API (application programmer interface) is a collection of dynamic link libraries (.DLL files) that contain Windows system functions you can call if you provide a declaration for Visual Basic in a .BAS file. These declarations are available for you in the *Win 3.1 API Help* Windows Help file that comes with Visual Basic Professional 3.0.

Tip

Storing information about your application in an .INI file is a very good idea because it is a common approach under Windows; as such, many Windows users and support professionals are familiar with them. On the other hand, it is a very *bad* idea to add application-specific items to the WIN.INI file, although many applications do so. Microsoft applications are the worst violators of this rule.

Every time an item is added to WIN.INI, it slows Windows down slightly, and it makes it much more difficult for a user to remove all traces of a program from their computer after they do not need it any longer.

To create or update a *private* .INI file, one that you name yourself, you call the WritePrivateProfileString function. To read the values from a *private* .INI file, you call the GetPrivateProfileString function.

To update a WIN.INI file, you call the WriteProfileString function and to read the values from WIN.INI, you call the GetProfileString function.

The declarations for the four profile string functions are contained in Listing 10.14.

Listing 10.14 Declarations for Windows API functions for processing .INI files.

```
'Write to Private .INI file
Declare Function WritePrivateProfileString
➥Lib "Kernel" (ByVal AppName$, ByVal
➥KeyName$, ByVal KeyValues$, ByVal
➥FileName$) As Integer

'Read from Private .INI file
Declare Function GetPrivateProfileString Lib
➥"Kernel" (ByVal AppName$, ByVal KeyName$,
➥ByVal Defaults$, ByVal ReturnedKeyValues$,
➥ByVal nSize As Integer, ByVal FileName$) As Integer

'Write to WIN.INI file
Declare Function WriteProfileString Lib
➥"Kernel" (ByVal AppName$, KeyName$,
➥KeyValues$) As Integer
```

```
'Read from WIN.INI file
Declare Function GetProfileString Lib
➥"Kernel" (ByVal AppName$, KeyName$, ByVal
➥Default$, ByVal ReturnedString$, ByVal nSize
ÂAs Integer) As Integer
```

Listing 10.15 shows you how to call the two functions
`WritePrivateProfileString` and `GetPrivateProfileString`.

**Listing 10.15 Calling the Windows API functions for processing
.INI files.**

```
Dim n As Integer
Dim TestValue As String * 5
n = WritePrivateProfileString("myapp",
➥"test", "ABCDE", "myapp.ini")
n = GetPrivateProfileString("myapp",
➥"test", "", TestValue, 5, "myapp.ini")
MsgBox(TextValue) 'Should display ABCDE
```

From Here...

As you have learned, you can store information to disk files and later read
that information back into your programs using Visual Basic's file commands.
As far as Visual Basic is concerned, there are three types of files: sequential,
random, and binary.

You also learned the following information in this chapter:

- To gain access to a disk file, you use the `Open` statement.

- Whenever you open a file, you should include error-handling code in
  case an error occurs.

- You can read information from a file using the `Input$` function.

- You can determine the length of an open file using the `Lof` function.

- The `FreeFile` function returns the next unused file number and makes
  your routines that open files more generic.

- You read sequential files with the `Line Input` or `Input` statements, and
  you write to them using `Print#` or `Write#`.

- You declare records for random-access files using `Type...End Type`.

■ You read random and binary files with the Get statement, and you write to them using the Put statement.

■ Random-access files can be used for creating simple databases.

■ You can move the file pointer in a random or binary file using the Seek statement, and you retrieve the current position with the Seek function (and the last byte position processed with the Loc function).

■ You can read and update .INI files by calling routines from the Windows API.

Index

Symbols

$ (dollar sign) data type suffix, 75
* (asterisk) multiplication operator, 81
+ (plus sign) addition operator, 81
- (minus sign) subtraction operator, 81
/ (slash) division operator, 82
< (less than) comparison operator, 84
<= (less than or equal to) comparison operator, 84
<> (not equal) comparison operator, 84
= (equal sign) comparison operator, 84
> (greater than) comparison operator, 84
>= (greater than or equal to) comparison operator, 84
\ (backslash) integer division operator, 82-83
^ (caret) exponentiation operator, 82-83
… (ellipsis) in commands, 10

A

Abs function, 118-119
ActiveControl property, 33
Add File command (File menu), 14
Add Watch command (Debug menu), 188
AddItem method, 63
addition operator (+), 81

Alignment property (controls), 67-68
American Standard Code for Information Interchange (ASCII), 107
AND operator, 87
ANSI (American National Standards Institute), 107
arithmetic operators, 81-84
arrays, 141-142
    bounds, 147-148
    counting, 150-151
    declaring, 143
    dimensions, 148-150
    multidimensional arrays, 144-146
    searching, 151-152
    sizing, 144
    sorting, 152
        QuickSort, 154-155
        substitution sort, 153
    user-defined data types, 146-147
ArryDimensions function, 148-150
Asc function, 109
ASCII (American Standard Code for Information Interchange), 107
    text files, 194-196
        reading, 203
        writing to, 205
assigning projects to groups, 28-29
asterisk (*) multiplication operator, 81
attaching code, 25-27
AUTOEXEC.BAT file, 206-207

B

BackColor property, 34
backslash (\) integer division operator, 82-83
Beep function, 120-121
binary files, 218-219
    current position, 217
    opening, 215
    reading, 216
    updating position, 216-217
    writing, 216
binary format (saving files), 20
binary numbers, 105-108
bitmaps, 41
.BMP file format, 41
BorderColor property, 34
BorderStyle property, 38-39
bounds (arrays), 147-148
breakpoints, 185-187
bugs
    logic-related, 176
    operation-related, 176-178
    prevention, 178-179
    see also debugging
    syntax-related, 176
buttons (message boxes), 162-163

C

calculator control
    attaching code, 25-27
    creating, 22-27
    editing, 43
    interface, 23
    opening, 42
    running, 27, 44
    saving, 28

Caption property, 25, 36, 64-65
caret (^) exponentiation operator, 82-83
Case Else clause, 131
check boxes, 56
Chr$ function, 110
Clear method, 64
Click events, 26
Close statement, 201-202
closing files, 201-202
Code window, 26
Color Palette command (Window menu), 35
color properties, 34-36
combo boxes, 61
command buttons, 53-54, 103
commands
    … (ellipsis), 10
    Debug menu
        Add Watch, 188
        Edit Watch, 190
        Single Step, 182
        Toggle Breakpoint, 186
    Edit menu
        Copy, 52
        Paste, 52
    File menu
        Add File, 14
        Exit, 28
        Make EXE File, 27
        New Form, 31
        New Project, 22
        Open Project, 42
        Remove File, 13
        Save Project, 28
    Help menu
        Contents, 16
        How to Use Help, 19
        Search for Help On, 17
    Options menu
        Environment, 20
        Project, 21
    Run menu, 27
    TYPE, 195
    Window menu
        Color Palette, 35
        Properties, 32
        Toolbox, 47
comparing strings, 108
comparison operators, 84-86
conditional statements, 125
    If…Then, 126-129
    Select Case, 129-131
    Switch function, 131-132

Contents command (Help menu), 16
control menu, 39-40
ControlBox property, 40
controls, 53
    attaching code, 25-27
    check boxes, 56
    combo boxes, 61
    command buttons, 53-54
    copying, 52-53
    creating, 22-27
    custom controls, 13
    DateDiff function, 102
    deleting, 53
    drawing, 14, 48
    frame control, 57-59
    grouping, 57-59
    interfaces, 23
    labels, 54-55
    list boxes, 60
    methods, 62-64
    moving, 51
    option buttons, 56-57
    pasting, 52
    properties
        Alignment, 67-68
        Caption, 64-65
        changing, 49-51
        DateDiff function, 102
        Enabled, 68
        FontName, 66
        TabIndex, 69
        Text, 65
        text box, 65-66
        Value, 68
        Visible, 68-69
    regular controls, 12-13
    running projects, 27
    saving, 28
    scroll bars, 59-60
    selecting, 49
    sizing, 15, 51-52
    text boxes, 55
    Toolbox, 48
    values, 51
converting strings, 109-111
Copy command (Edit menu), 52
copying
    controls, 52-53
    files, 207
counting, 150-151
Currency data type, 75
current time, 96-97
custom controls, 13

D

Data Interchange Format (.DIF) files, 197
data types, 71-73
    $ (dollar sign), 75
    Currency, 75
    Date/Time, 76
    Double, 74-75
    Empty, 77
    Integer, 73
    IsEmpty function, 77
    Long, 73
    see also variables
    Single, 74
    Strings, 75-76
    user-defined, 146-147
    variable declaration, 77
        Dim statement, 78
        Global statement, 79-81
        Option Explicit, 78
        Static statement, 79
    Variant, 76
Date functions, 94
    storing, 95-96
    today's date, 96
Date/Time data type, 76
DateAdd function, 104-105
DateDiff function, 100-104
Day function, 99-100
Debug menu commands
    Add Watch, 188
    Edit Watch, 190
    Single Step, 182
    Toggle Breakpoint, 186
debugging
    breakpoints, 185-187
    Instant Watch tool, 188-191
    logic-related errors, 176
    operation-related errors, 176-177
    preventing bugs, 178-179
    single stepping, 182-185
    syntax-related errors, 176
declaring arrays, 143
default input (input boxes), 168
Define Color dialog box, 35
defining records (random-access files), 210-212
deleting
    breakpoints, 187
    controls, 53
    custom controls, 13
    files, 207

delimited text files, 208-219
dialog boxes
    creating, 169-170
    Define Color, 35
    displaying, 172-173
    options, 170-171
    screen location, 171-172
    see also message boxes
.DIB file format, 41
.DIF (Data Interchange
    Format) files, 197
Dim statement, 78
displaying custom dialog
    boxes, 172-173
division operator (/), 82
.DLL files, 220
Do...Loop loops, 134-136
DoEvents function, 121-123
dollar sign ($) data type
    suffix, 75
Double data type, 74-75
drawing controls, 14, 48
Dropdown Combo boxes, 61
Dropdown lists, 62
dynamic link library (.DLL)
    files, 220

E

Edit menu commands, 52
Edit Watch command (Debug
    menu), 190
ellipsis (...) in commands, 10
ElseIf...Then clause, 127
Empty data type, 77
Enabled property (controls),
    68
encrypting text, 110
environment, customizing,
    20-21
Environment command
    (Options menu), 20
Eof function, 204
equal sign (=) comparison
    operator, 84
EQV operator, 88
Erase statement, 145
Err function, 200
errors
    file errors, 200
    logic-related, 176
    operation-related, 176-177
    syntax-related, 176
events, 26

executable files, 44
executing, *see* running
Exit command (File menu), 28
Exit Do statement, 134
exiting
    loops, 135-136
    Visual Basic, 28
exponentiation operator (^),
    82-83
export file formats, 196-197
extracting
    date, 99
    ends of strings, 114
    integers, 116
    middle of strings, 115

F

File menu commands
    Add File, 14
    Exit, 28
    Make EXE File, 27
    New Form, 31
    New Project, 22
    Open Project, 42
    Remove File, 13
    Save Project, 28
FileCopy statement, 207
files
    AUTOEXEC.BAT, 206-207
    binary
        current position, 217
        opening, 215
        reading, 216
        saving, 20
        updating position,
            216-217
        writing, 216
    closing, 201-202
    copying, 207
    deleting, 207
    errors, 200
    executable, 44
    formats
        .BMP, 41
        .DIB, 41
        .FRM, 204-205
        .ICO, 41
        .WMF, 41
    .INI (initialization) files
        private, 220-221
        updating, 219-221
    length, 201
    loading, 202
    opening, 198-199

random-access, 209
    defining records, 210-212
    opening, 212
    reading records, 213
    writing, 214-215
reading data files, 200-201
saving, 20
sequential, 203-209
SYSTEM.INI, 219
types, 193
    ASCII text files, 194-196
    foreign file formats, 196
    import/export formats,
        196-197
    .INI files, 197
FillColor property, 34
FontName property (controls),
    66
fonts, 66-67
For...Next loops, 98, 136-139,
    151
ForeColor property, 34
foreign file formats, 196
Format function, 119
formatting
    forms, 32
    If...Then structures, 127
    output, 119
    text, 67
    user prompts (InputBox$),
        167
forms, 7-8
    adding, 31
    controls, 102
    date calculator, 103
    dialog boxes
        creating, 169-170
        displaying, 172-173
        options, 170-171
        screen location, 171-172
    formatting, 32
    properties, 32
        BorderStyle, 38-39
        color, 34-36
        control menu, 39-40
        DateDiff function, 102
        Icon, 40
        location, 37-38
        size, 37-38
        text, 36-37
        types, 33
        Visible, 39
        WindowState, 42
FreeFile function, 199
.FRM files, 204-205
function keys, 10

functions, 93-94
    Abs, 118-119
    ArryDimensions, 148-150
    Asc, 109
    Beep, 120-121
    Chr$, 110
    Date/Time, 94
        accuracy, 95
        current time, 96-97
        storing, 95-96
        today's date, 96
    DateAdd, 104-105
    DateDiff, 100-104
    Day, 99-100
    DoEvents, 121-123
    Eof, 204
    Err, 200
    Format, 119
    FreeFile, 199
    Hour, 101
    Input$, 200
    InputBox$, 165
        default input, 168
        prompts, 166-167
        screen location, 169
        titles, 167-168
    InStr, 114
    Int, 116
    IsDate, 104
    IsEmpty, 77
    LBound, 148
    LCase, 109
    Left$, 114
    Len, 113
    LoadFile, 202
    Loc, 217
    Lof, 200
    math functions, 115-119
    Mid$, 115
    Minute, 101
    Month, 99-100
    MsgBox, 104, 163
    Now, 97-99
    Randomize, 117
    Right$, 114
    Rnd, 116-117
    Second, 101
    Seek, 217
    Sgn, 118
    Space, 112-113
    Str$, 111
    StrComp, 108
    String$, 112
    strings, 105-108
    Switch, 131-132
    UBound, 148

    UCase, 109
    Val, 111-117
    Weekday, 99-100
    WritePrivateProfileString, 220-221
    Year, 99-100

G

Get# statement, 213
Global statement, 79-81, 143
GoTo statements, 139-140
greater than (>) comparison operator, 84
greater than or equal to (>=) comparison operator, 84
grouping, 57-59
grouping controls, 57-59
groups, assigning projects, 28-29

H

hardware system requirements, 5-6
Height property, 38
help, 16
    navigating, 18-19
    SAMPLES subdirectory, 19
    searching, 17-18
    tutorial, 19
Help menu commands
    Contents, 16
    How to Use Help, 19
    Search for Help On, 17
Hide method, 172
horizontal scroll bars control, 59
Hour function, 101
How to Use Help command (Help menu), 19

I

.ICO file format, 41
Icon property, 40
icons (message boxes), 161-163
If...Then loops, 151
If...Then statements, 126-129
IMP operator, 90
import file formats, 196-197

incrementing loop counters, 137
indentation of nested If statements, 128
.INI (initialization) files, 197
    private .INI files, 220-221
    updating, 219-221
Input# statement, 208
Input$, 200
InputBox$ function, 165
    default input, 168
    prompts, 166-167
    screen location, 169
    titles, 167-168
installation, 6
Instant Watch tool, 188-191
InStr function, 114
Int function, 116
Integer data type, 73
integer division operator (\), 82-83
integers, extracting, 116
interfaces, 23
IsDate function, 104
IsEmpty function, 77

K–L

keyboard, 8-9
Kill statement, 207
labels, 54-55
LBound functions, 148
LCase function, 109
Left Property, 37
Left$ function, 114
Len function, 113
less than (<) comparison operator, 84
less than or equal to (<=) comparison operator, 84
list boxes, 60
listings
    4.1 spelling errors, 78
    4.2 AND operator, 87
    4.3 EQV operator, 88
    4.4 OR operator, 89
    4.5 XOR operator, 90
    4.6 IMP operator, 90
    4.7 NOT operator, 90
    5.1 timing project execution, 97
    5.2 Weekday function, 99
    5.3 date calculator command button, 103

5.4 date calculator form, 103
5.5 string conversion, 109
5.6 encrypting text, 110
5.7 beep length, 120
5.8 beep frequency, 120
5.9 code without DoEvents, 121
5.10 code with DoEvents, 122
5.11 placing DoEvents, 123
6.1 nested Ifs, 128
6.2 nested Ifs, 128-130
6.3 nested Ifs, 128-130
6.4 If statement without Not operator, 129
6.5 If statements with Not operator, 129
6.6 If...Then code determining digits, 129-130
6.7 Select Case statement, 131-133
6.8 Switch statement, 131-133
6.9 Do...Loop statement, 135
6.10 Do...Loop statement, 135
6.11 Exit Do statement, 135-136
6.12 For...Next statement, 136
6.13 Do...Loop equivalent to For...Next, 137
6.14 incrementing loop counters, 137
6.15 For...Step...Next statement, 138
6.16 nested For...Next loops, 138
6.17 DoEvents with For...Next loops, 139
6.18 GoTo statement, 140
6.19 GoTo statement with labels, 140
7.1 type declaration, 147
7.2 array dimensions, 149-150
7.3 searching arrays, 152-155
7.4 substitution sorts (arrays), 153-155
7.5 QuickSort (arrays), 154-155
8.1 dialog boxes, 159
8.2 MsgBox statement, 159
8.3 long messages, 160

8.4 dialog boxes with titles, 160
8.5 message box icons, 161
8.6 message box buttons, 162
8.7 icon and button types (message boxes), 163
8.8 modal dialog boxes, 165
8.9 InputBox$, 166
8.10 formatting user prompts (InputBox$), 167
8.11 input box titles, 168
8.12 default input (InputBox$), 168
8.13 form centering, 172
9.1 code with bugs, 180-191
9.2 code after debugging, 185
10.1 delimited text files, 197
10.2 file errors, 200
10.3 reading files, 201
10.4 loading files, 202
10.5 loading declarations from .FRM files, 204-205
10.6 fixing PATH statement, 206-207
10.7 updating AUTOEXEC.BAT file, 208
10.8 user info records, 212
10.9 Get# statement, 213-214
10.10 Get# statement, 214-215
10.11 Seek statement, 217
10.12 saving byte positions, 218
10.13 SYSTEM.INI file, 219
10.14 declarations for Windows API functions, 220-221
10.15 calling Windows API functions, 221
Load statement, 173
LoadFile file, 202
loading files, 202
Loc function, 217
location properties, 37-38
Lof function, 200
logic-related errors, 176
logical operators, 86-90
Long data type, 73
looping structures, 132
    Do...Loop, 134-136
    For...Next, 98, 136-139, 151
    If...Then, 151
    While...Wend, 133

M

Make EXE File command (File menu), 27
math functions, 115
    Abs, 118-119
    Format, 119
    Int, 116
    Randomize, 117
    Rnd, 116-117
    Sgn, 118
MaxButton property, 39
MaxLength property (controls), 65
menu bars, 8-10
message boxes, 157-158
    buttons, 162-163
    combining icons and buttons, 163
    icons, 161-163
    input boxes
        default input, 168
        prompts, 166-167
        screen location, 169
        titles, 167-168
    modality, 164-165
    MsgBox statement, 158-160
    titles, 160
    user response, 163-164
methods, 62-64
    Hide, 172
    Show, 172
Mid$ function, 115
MinButton property, 39
minus sign (-) subtraction operator, 81
Minute function, 101
Mod operator, 82-84
modality (message boxes), 164-165
Month function, 99-100
mouse, 8
moving controls, 51
MsgBox function, 104, 163
MsgBox statement, 158-160
multidimensional arrays, 144-146
multiplication operator (*), 81

N

Name property, 25, 36
navigating help, 18-19
nested For...Next statements, 138
nested If statements, 128
New Form command (File menu), 31
New Project command (File menu), 22
NOT comparison operator, 129
not equa (<>) comparison operator, 84
NOT operator, 90
Now function, 97-99

O

objects (Screen), 171-172
On Error Resume Next, 200
Open Project command (File menu), 42
Open statement, 198
opening
    binary files, 215
    calculator control, 42
    files, 198-199
    random-access files, 212
operation-related errors, 176-177
operators
    arithmetic, 81-84
    comparison, 84-86
    logical, 86-90
    string, 91
Option Base statement, 150-151
option buttons, 56-57
Option Explicit statement, 78
Options menu commands, 20-21
OR operator, 88-89

P

PasswordChar property (controls), 65
Paste command (Edit menu), 52
pasting controls, 52
PATH settings, 206-207

plus sign (+) addition operator, 81
private .INI files, 220-221
programs, *see* projects
Project command (Options menu), 21
Project options, 21-22
Project window, 11-12
projects, 22
    assigning to groups, 28-29
    attaching code, 25-27
    calculator control, 42-44
    creating, 22-27
    formatting output, 119
    forms, 31-33
    interfaces, 23
    properties, 49
    running, 27
    saving, 28
    timing execution, 97
prompts (input boxes), 166-167
properties, 32-34
    ActiveControl, 33
    BorderStyle, 38-39
    Caption, 25, 36
    color, 34-36
    control menu, 39-40
    ControlBox, 40
    controls
        Alignment, 67-68
        Caption, 64-65
        changing, 49-51
        DateDiff function, 102
        Enabled, 68
        FontName, 66
        TabIndex, 69
        Text, 65
        text box, 65-66
        Value, 68
        Visible, 68-69
    forms, 102
    Height, 38
    Icon, 40
    Left, 37
    location, 37-38
    MaxLength, 65
    Name, 25, 36
    PasswordChar, 65
    size, 37-38
    text, 36-37
    Top, 37
    types, 33
    Visible, 39
    Width, 38
    WindowState, 42

Properties command (Window menu), 32
Properties window, 15, 32
Put statement, 214-215

Q–R

QuickSort (arrays), 154-155
random numbers, 116-117
random-access files
    defining records, 210-212
    opening, 212
    reading records, 213
    versus sequential, 209-210
    writing, 214-215
Randomize function, 117
reading
    ASCII text files, 203
    binary files, 216
    data files, 200-201
    delimited text files, 208
    random-access files, 213
ReDim statement, 144
regular controls, 12-13
Remove File command (File menu), 13
RemoveItem method, 63
resizing, *see* sizing
Rich Text Format (.RTF) files, 197
Right$ function, 114
Rnd function, 116-117
.RTF (Rich Text Format) files, 197
Run menu commands, 27
running projects, 27, 44, 49

S

SAMPLES subdirectory, 19
Save Project command (File menu), 28
saving
    byte positions, 218
    files, 20
    projects, 28
Screen object, 171-172
scroll bars, 59-60
Search for Help On command (Help menu), 17
searching
    arrays, 151-152
    help, 17-18

Second function, 101
Seek function, 217
Seek statement, 216-217
Select Case statements, 129-131
selecting controls, 49
sequential files, 203-210
Sgn function, 118
shortcut keys, 9
Show method, 172
Simple Combo boxes, 62
Single data type, 74
Single Step command (Debug menu), 182
single stepping, 182-185
size properties, 37-38
sizing
    arrays, 144
    controls, 15, 51-52
slash (/) division operator, 82
software system requirements, 5-6
sorting arrays, 152-155
sound, 120-121
Space function, 112-113
Start command (Run menu), 27
starting Visual Basic, 6-7
statements
    Close, 201-202
    conditional statements, 125
        If...Then, 126-129
        Select Case, 129-131
        Switch function, 131-132
    Dim, 78
    Erase, 145
    Exit Do, 134
    FileCopy, 207
    Get#, 213
    Global, 79-81, 143
    GoTo, 139-140
    Input#, 208
    Kill, 207
    Load, 173
    looping structures
        Do...Loop, 134-136
        For...Next, 136-139, 151
        If...Then, 151
        While...Wend, 133
    MsgBox, 158-160
    Open, 198
    Option Base, 150-151
    Option Explicit, 78
    Put, 214-215
    ReDim, 144

Seek, 216-217
Static, 79, 143
Type, 146
Type...End Type, 210
Unload, 173
Write#, 208-219
Static statement, 79, 143
Str$ function, 111
StrComp function, 108
string operators, 91
String$ function, 112
Strings, 75-76
strings
    case, 109
    comparing, 108
    converting, 109-111
    creating, 112-113
    extracting ends, 114
    extracting middle, 115
    functions, 105-108
        Asc, 109
        Chr$, 110
        InStr, 114
        LCase, 109
        Left$, 114
        Len, 113
        Mid$, 115
        Right$, 114
        Space, 112-113
        Str$, 111
        StrComp, 108
        String$, 112
        UCase, 109
        Val, 111-117
    length, 113
substitution sort (arrays), 153
subtraction operator (-), 81
Switch function, 131-132
syntax-related errors, 176
system requirements, 5-6
SYSTEM.INI file, 219

T

TabIndex property (controls), 69
TabStop property (controls), 69
text
    encryption, 110
    FontName property, 66
    formatting, 67
    properties, 36-37
text boxes, 55, 65-66

Text property, 65
Time functions, 94
    accuracy, 95
    current time, 96-97
    storing, 95-96
timing project execution, 97
titles (InputBox$ function), 167-168
titles (message boxes), 160
today's date, 96
Toggle Breakpoint command (Debug menu), 186
Toolbars, 10-11
Toolbox, 12-15, 47-48
    check boxes, 56
    combo boxes, 61
    command buttons, 53-54
    frame control, 57-59
    grouping, 57-59
    labels, 54-55
    list boxes, 60
    option buttons, 56-57
    scroll bars, 59-60
    text boxes, 55
Toolbox command (Window menu), 47
Top property, 37
TrueType fonts, 66
truth tables
    AND, 87
    EQV, 88
    IMP, 90
    OR, 88
    XOR, 89
tutorial, 19
TYPE command, 195
Type statement, 146
Type...End Type statement, 210

U

UBound function, 148
UCase function, 109
Unload statement, 173
user response (message boxes), 163-164
user-defined data types, 146-147

V

Val function, 111-117
Value property (controls), 68
variables, 71-73
    $ (dollar sign), 75
    Currency, 75
    Date/Time, 76
    declaration, 77
        Dim statement, 78
        Global statement, 79-81
        Option Explicit, 78
        Static statement, 79
    Double, 74-75
    Empty, 77
    Integer, 73
    IsEmpty function, 77
    Long, 73
    operators
        arithmetic, 81-84
        comparison, 84-86
        logical, 86-90
        string, 91
    Single, 74
    Strings, 75-76
    Variant, 76
Variant data type, 76
vertical scroll bar control, 59
Visible property, 39, 68-69
Visual Basic
    customizing, 20-22
    exiting, 28

W

watch expressions, 188-191
Weekday function, 99-100
While...Wend loops, 133
Width property, 38
Window menu commands
    Color Palette, 35
    Properties, 32
    Toolbox, 47
Windows, 121-123
windows
    Code, 26
    components, 7-15
    forms, 7-8
    menu bars, 8-10
    Project, 11-12
    Properties, 15, 32
    Toolbars, 10-11
    Toolbox, 12-15
Windows API, 220-222
WindowState property, 42
.WMF file format, 41
Write# statement, 208-219
WritePrivateProfileString
  function, 220-221
writing
    binary files, 216
    delimited text files, 208-219
    random-access files, 214-215
    to ASCII text files, 205

X–Y–Z

XOR operator, 89-90
Year function, 99-100